HEALTHY
MEDITERRANEAN
RECIPES

Publications International, Ltd.

Photographs on front cover and pages 99, 125, 149 and 181 copyright © Shutterstock.com.

Pictured on the front cover *(clockwise from top left):* Greek Salad *(page 44),* Hummus *(page 18),* Spiced Chicken Skewers with Yogurt-Tahini Sauce *(page 138)* and Pasta with Roasted Tomatoes and Feta *(page 98).*

Pictured on the back cover *(clockwise from top):* Chicken Cassoulet *(page 119),* Broiled Salmon with Cucumber Yogurt *(page 120),* Quick Greek Pitas *(page 145)* and Tirokafteri (Spicy Greek Feta Spread) *(page 22).*

ISBN: 978-1-64558-897-9

Manufactured in China.

8 7 6 5 4 3 2 1

Microwave Cooking: Microwave ovens vary in wattage. Use the cooking times as guidelines and check for doneness before adding more time.

Let's get social!
⊙ @Publications_International
f @PublicationsInternational
www.pilbooks.com

TABLE OF
CONTENTS

PER SERVING
calories *230*
total fat *20g*
saturated fat *10g*
carbs *5g*
dietary fiber *0g*
protein *8g*

SMALL PLATES
& SNACKS

Mediterranean Baked Feta

1 block (8 ounces) feta cheese, cut crosswise into 4 slices

½ cup grape tomatoes, halved

¼ cup sliced roasted red peppers

¼ cup pitted kalamata olives

⅛ teaspoon dried oregano

Black pepper

2 tablespoons extra virgin olive oil

1 tablespoon shredded fresh basil

Pita chips or toasted French bread slices (optional)

1. Preheat oven to 400°F.

2. Place cheese in small baking dish; top with tomatoes, roasted peppers and olives. Sprinkle with oregano and season with black pepper; drizzle with oil.

3. Bake 12 minutes or until cheese is soft. Sprinkle with basil. Serve immediately with pita chips, if desired.

French-Style Pizza Bites (Pissaladière)

MAKES ABOUT 24 SERVINGS (2 PIECES PER SERVING)

2 tablespoons extra virgin olive oil

2 medium onions, thinly sliced

1 medium red bell pepper, cut into thin strips

2 cloves garlic, minced

⅓ cup pitted black olives, quartered

1 can (about 14 ounces) refrigerated pizza crust dough

1 cup (4 ounces) finely shredded Swiss or Gruyère cheese

1. Move oven rack to lowest position. Preheat oven to 425°F. Grease large baking sheet.

2. Heat oil in medium skillet over medium heat. Add onions, bell pepper and garlic; cook and stir 5 minutes or until vegetables are crisp-tender. Stir in olives; remove from heat.

3. Pat dough into 16×12-inch rectangle on prepared baking sheet. Arrange vegetables over dough; sprinkle with cheese. Bake 10 minutes. Loosen crust from baking sheet; slide crust onto oven rack. Bake 3 to 5 minutes or until golden brown.

4. Slide pizza back onto baking sheet; transfer to cutting board. Cut pizza crosswise into eight 1¾-inch-wide strips; cut diagonally into ten 2-inch-wide strips, making diamond pieces. Serve immediately.

Beans and Greens Crostini

MAKES ABOUT 24 CROSTINI (2 CROSTINI PER SERVING)

4 tablespoons extra virgin olive oil, divided

1 small onion, thinly sliced

4 cups thinly sliced Italian black kale or other dinosaur kale variety

2 tablespoons minced garlic, divided

1 tablespoon balsamic vinegar

2 teaspoons salt, divided

¼ teaspoon red pepper flakes

1 can (about 15 ounces) cannellini beans, rinsed and drained

1 tablespoon chopped fresh rosemary

1 loaf French bread, cut into 24 thin slices, toasted

1. Heat 1 tablespoon oil in large skillet over medium heat. Add onion; cook and stir 5 minutes or until softened. Add kale and 1 tablespoon garlic; cook 15 minutes or until kale is softened and most liquid has evaporated, stirring occasionally. Stir in vinegar, 1 teaspoon salt and red pepper flakes.

2. Meanwhile, combine beans, remaining 3 tablespoons oil, 1 tablespoon garlic, 1 teaspoon salt and rosemary in food processor or blender; process until smooth.

3. Spread bean mixture over bread slices; top with kale.

PER SERVING
calories *190*
total fat *6g*
saturated fat *1g*
carbs *26g*
dietary fiber *2g*
protein *7g*

Mini Chickpea Cakes

MAKES 24 CAKES (3 CAKES PER SERVING)

1 can (about 15 ounces)
  chickpeas, rinsed and
  drained

1 cup shredded carrots

⅓ cup seasoned dry bread
  crumbs

¼ cup reduced-fat creamy Italian
  salad dressing

1 egg

1. Preheat oven to 375°F. Grease large baking sheet.

2. Mash chickpeas coarsely with potato masher in large mixing bowl. Stir in carrots, bread crumbs, salad dressing and egg; mix well.

3. Shape mixture into 24 small patties; place on prepared baking sheet.

4. Bake 15 to 18 minutes or until patties are lightly browned on both sides, turning once halfway through baking. Serve warm.

PER SERVING
calories *102*
total fat *2g*
saturated fat *1g*
carbs *17g*
dietary fiber *3g*
protein *4g*

Paprika-Spiced Almonds

MAKES ABOUT 8 SERVINGS (2 TABLESPOONS PER SERVING)

1 cup whole blanched almonds

¾ teaspoon olive oil

¼ teaspoon coarse salt

¼ teaspoon smoked paprika or sweet paprika

1. Preheat oven to 375°F. Spread almonds in single layer in shallow baking pan. Bake 8 to 10 minutes or until almonds are lightly browned. Transfer to small bowl; cool 5 minutes.

2. Add oil to almonds; stir until coated. Sprinkle with salt and paprika; stir to coat.

TIP: For the best flavor, serve these almonds the day they are made.

PER SERVING
calories *110*
total fat *10g*
saturated fat *1g*
carbs *4g*
dietary fiber *2g*
protein *4g*

Onion and White Bean Spread

MAKES 1¼ CUPS SPREAD (2 TABLESPOONS SPREAD AND 1 BREAD SLICE PER SERVING)

1 can (about 15 ounces) cannellini or Great Northern beans, rinsed and drained

¼ cup chopped green onions

¼ cup grated Parmesan cheese

¼ cup extra virgin olive oil, plus additional for serving

1 tablespoon fresh rosemary, chopped

2 cloves garlic, minced

10 French bread slices, toasted

1. Combine beans, green onions, cheese, ¼ cup oil, rosemary and garlic in food processor; process 30 to 40 seconds or until almost smooth.

2. Spoon bean mixture into serving bowl. Drizzle additional oil over spread just before serving. Serve with bread.

TIP: For a more rustic-looking spread, place all ingredients in a medium bowl and mash them with a potato masher.

PER SERVING
calories *190*
total fat *7g*
saturated fat *2g*
carbs *25g*
dietary fiber *2g*
protein *8g*

Simple Bruschetta

MAKES 4 SERVINGS (¼ CUP TOPPING AND 2 BREAD SLICES)

1 tablespoon extra virgin olive oil

2 tablespoons thinly sliced red onion

1 clove garlic, minced

1 cup chopped seeded tomatoes

¼ teaspoon salt

⅛ teaspoon black pepper

8 thin French bread slices, toasted or grilled

¼ cup slivered fresh basil

1. Heat oil in medium skillet over medium heat. Add onion; cook and stir 3 minutes. Add garlic; cook and stir 1 minute.

2. Stir in tomatoes, salt and pepper; let stand 10 minutes. Serve mixture on bread slices; sprinkle with basil.

PER SERVING
calories *140*
total fat *5g*
saturated fat *1g*
carbs *21g*
dietary fiber *1g*
protein *4g*

Hummus

MAKES ABOUT 3¼ CUPS (¼ CUP PER SERVING)

8 ounces dried chickpeas, rinsed and sorted

6 cups water

1 tablespoon plus ½ teaspoon salt, divided

¼ cup lemon juice

2 cloves garlic, smashed

¼ teaspoon ground cumin

½ cup tahini

1 cup cold water, divided

2 tablespoons extra virgin olive oil, plus additional for serving

Chopped fresh parsley (optional)

Za'atar or paprika (optional)

1. Place chickpeas in medium bowl; cover with water. Soak 8 hours or overnight.

2. Drain chickpeas; place in medium saucepan. Add 6 cups water and 1 tablespoon salt. Bring to a boil over high heat. Reduce heat to medium-low; simmer 40 to 45 minutes or until chickpeas are tender, skimming foam. Drain.

3. Combine lemon juice, garlic, remaining ½ teaspoon salt and cumin in bowl of food processor; let stand 5 minutes. Add tahini and ¼ cup cold water; process until well blended. Add cooked chickpeas, 2 tablespoons oil and ⅓ cup cold water; process about 3 minutes or until very smooth, stopping to scrape down side of bowl once or twice. Add additional cold water, 1 tablespoon at a time, if necessary to thin hummus.

4. Top with additional oil, parsley and za'atar or paprika, if desired.

TIP: To save time, use 2 cans (about 15 ounces each) chickpeas, rinsed and drained, instead of the dried chickpeas. Skip steps 1 and 2 and proceed as directed with step 3.

Baba Ganoush

MAKES ABOUT 2½ CUPS (¼ CUP PER SERVING)

2 medium eggplants (about 1 pound each)

¼ cup tahini

2 tablespoons lemon juice

1½ tablespoons dark sesame oil, divided

1 clove garlic, minced

1 teaspoon salt

¼ teaspoon black pepper

Chopped fresh parsley

Extra virgin olive oil (optional)

Pita bread, cut into wedges

1. Prepare grill for direct cooking. Prick eggplants in several places with fork. Place eggplants on grid. Grill, covered, over medium-high heat 30 to 40 minutes or until skin is black and blistered and pulp is soft, turning often. Peel eggplants when cool enough to handle. Let cool to room temperature.

2. Transfer eggplants to medium bowl; mash with potato masher until no large pieces remain.* Add tahini, lemon juice, sesame oil, garlic, salt and pepper; stir until well blended. Garnish with parsley; drizzle with olive oil, if desired. Serve with pita.

*For a smoother dip, transfer cooked eggplant to food processor. Add tahini, lemon juice, sesame oil, garlic, salt and pepper; process until smooth.

Tirokafteri
(Spicy Greek Feta Spread)

MAKES 2 CUPS (2 TABLESPOONS PER SERVING)

2 small hot red peppers

½ small clove garlic

1 block (8 ounces) feta cheese

¾ cup plain Greek yogurt

1 tablespoon lemon juice

½ teaspoon salt

Toasted French bread slices and/or cut-up fresh vegetables

1. Preheat oven to 400°F. Place peppers on small piece of foil on baking sheet. Bake 15 minutes or until peppers are soft and charred. Cool completely. Scrape off skin with paring knife. Cut off top and remove seeds. Place peppers in food processor. Add garlic; pulse until finely chopped.

2. Add cheese, yogurt, lemon juice and salt; pulse until well blended but still chunky. Serve with bread, vegetables or cooked meats. Store in airtight jar in refrigerator up to 2 weeks.

PER SERVING

calories *45*

total fat *3g*

saturated fat *2g*

carbs *1g*

dietary fiber *0g*

protein *4g*

PER SERVING
calories *370*
total fat *13g*
saturated fat *5g*
carbs *45g*
dietary fiber *4g*
protein *25g*

SALADS
& VEGETABLES

Mediterranean Salad

MAKES 4 SERVINGS

2 cups chopped iceberg lettuce

2 cups baby spinach

2 cups diced cucumbers

1 cup diced cooked chicken

1 cup chopped roasted red peppers

1 cup grape tomatoes, halved

1 cup quartered artichoke hearts

¾ cup crumbled feta cheese

½ cup chopped red onion

1 cup hummus

½ teaspoon Italian seasoning

1. Divide lettuce and spinach among four salad bowls or plates; top with cucumbers, chicken, roasted peppers, tomatoes, artichokes, cheese and onion.

2. Top salad with hummus; sprinkle with Italian seasoning.

Parmesan Potato Wedges

MAKES 6 SERVINGS

2 pounds unpeeled red potatoes, cut into ½-inch wedges

¼ cup finely chopped yellow onion

1½ teaspoons dried oregano

½ teaspoon salt

Black pepper

2 tablespoons butter, cut into pieces or extra virgin olive oil

¼ cup grated Parmesan cheese

1. Preheat oven to 400°F. Spray large baking sheet with nonstick cooking spray. Spread potatoes on baking sheet; sprinkle with onion, oregano, salt and pepper. Dot with butter.

2. Bake 30 to 40 minutes or until potatoes are browned and tender, stirring once during baking. Transfer potatoes to serving platter; sprinkle with cheese.

Zucchini Chickpea Salad

MAKES 4 TO 6 SERVINGS

3 medium zucchini (about 6 ounces each)

½ teaspoon salt

5 tablespoons white vinegar

1 clove garlic, minced

¼ teaspoon dried thyme

½ cup extra virgin olive oil

1 cup drained canned chickpeas

½ cup sliced pitted black olives

3 green onions, minced

1 canned chipotle pepper in adobo sauce, seeded and minced

1 ripe avocado, cut into ½-inch cubes

⅓ cup crumbled feta cheese

Lettuce leaves and sliced fresh tomatoes (optional)

1. Cut zucchini lengthwise into halves; cut halves crosswise into ¼-inch-thick slices. Place slices in medium bowl; sprinkle with salt. Toss to mix. Spread zucchini on several layers of paper towels. Let stand at room temperature 30 minutes to drain.

2. Combine vinegar, garlic and thyme in large bowl. Gradually whisk in oil until well blended. Pat zucchini dry; add to dressing. Add chickpeas, olives and green onions; toss lightly to coat. Cover and refrigerate at least 30 minutes or up to 4 hours, stirring occasionally.

3. Stir in chipotle pepper; fold in avocado and cheese. Serve salad on lettuce with tomato slices, if desired.

PER SERVING
calories *310*
total fat *27g*
saturated fat *4g*
carbs *16g*
dietary fiber *6g*
protein *6g*

Summer Vegetable Bake

2 tomatoes, sliced

1 small red onion, sliced

1 medium zucchini, sliced

1 small eggplant, sliced

1 small yellow squash, sliced

1 large portobello mushroom, sliced

2 cloves garlic, finely chopped

3 tablespoons extra virgin olive oil

2 teaspoons chopped fresh rosemary

⅔ cup dry white wine

Salt and black pepper

1. Preheat oven to 350°F. Grease oval or 13×9-inch baking dish.

2. Arrange slices of vegetables in rows, alternating different types and overlapping slices in baking dish to make attractive arrangement; sprinkle evenly with garlic. Combine oil and rosemary in small bowl; drizzle over vegetables.

3. Pour wine over vegetables; season with salt and pepper. Cover loosely with foil. Bake 20 minutes. Uncover; bake 10 to 15 minutes or until vegetables are tender.

PER SERVING
calories *230*
total fat *11g*
saturated fat *2g*
carbs *25g*
dietary fiber *5g*
protein *4g*

Greek Chicken and Kalamata Rice Salad

MAKES 6 SERVINGS

1¾ cups water

1 cup uncooked long grain rice

1 teaspoon salt

2 cups diced cooked chicken

1 medium cucumber, peeled, seeded and chopped

1 cup packed spinach leaves, coarsely chopped

16 kalamata olives, pitted and coarsely chopped

1 package (2¼ ounces) pine nuts, toasted*

¼ cup chopped fresh parsley

1½ teaspoons dried oregano

⅛ teaspoon red pepper flakes

½ cup olive oil vinaigrette

4 ounces crumbled feta cheese

Sliced tomatoes (optional)

To toast pine nuts, spread in single layer in small heavy skillet. Cook over medium heat 1 to 2 minutes or until nuts are lightly browned, stirring frequently. Cool before using.

1. Bring water, rice and salt to a boil in medium saucepan. Reduce heat to low; cover and simmer about 15 minutes or until water is absorbed. Spread rice on large baking sheet; cool to room temperature.

2. Combine rice, chicken, cucumber, spinach, olives, pine nuts, parsley, oregano and red pepper flakes in large bowl. Add dressing; mix well. Add cheese; gently mix. Serve salad on sliced tomatoes, if desired.

PER SERVING
calories *510*
total fat *36g*
saturated fat *7g*
carbs *27g*
dietary fiber *2g*
protein *22g*

Beet and Arugula Salad

MAKES 6 SERVINGS

8 medium beets (5 to 6 ounces each)

⅓ cup red wine vinegar

¾ teaspoon salt

½ teaspoon black pepper

3 tablespoons extra virgin olive oil

1 package (5 ounces) baby arugula

1 package (4 ounces) crumbled goat cheese with garlic and herbs

1. Place beets in large saucepan; add water to cover by 2 inches. Bring to a boil over medium-high heat. Reduce heat to medium-low; cover and simmer 30 minutes or until beets can be easily pierced with tip of knife. Drain well; set aside until cool enough to handle.

2. Meanwhile, whisk vinegar, salt and pepper in large bowl. Slowly add oil in thin, steady stream, whisking until well blended. Remove 3 tablespoons dressing to medium bowl.

3. Peel beets and cut into wedges. Add warm beets to large bowl; toss to coat with dressing. Add arugula to medium bowl; toss gently to coat with dressing. Divide arugula among serving plates; top with beets and cheese.

PER SERVING
calories *170*
total fat *12g*
saturated fat *4g*
carbs *12g*
dietary fiber *3g*
protein *6g*

French Carrot Medley

2 cups sliced carrots

1 cup sliced mushrooms

¾ cup orange juice

4 stalks celery, sliced

¼ cup chopped onion

½ teaspoon dried dill weed

¼ cup cold water

2 teaspoons cornstarch

Salt and black pepper

1. Combine carrots, mushrooms, orange juice, celery, onion and dill in medium saucepan. Bring to a simmer over medium heat. Reduce heat to low; cover and simmer 12 minutes or until carrots are tender.

2. Stir water into cornstarch in small bowl until smooth. Stir into vegetable mixture; cook and stir until mixture thickens and bubbles. Season with salt and pepper.

PER SERVING
calories *42*
total fat *1g*
saturated fat *1g*
carbs *10g*
dietary fiber *2g*
protein *1g*

Broccoli Italian Style

MAKES 4 SERVINGS

1¼ pounds fresh broccoli

2 tablespoons lemon juice

1 teaspoon extra virgin olive oil

1 clove garlic, minced

1 teaspoon chopped fresh parsley

½ teaspoon salt

¼ teaspoon black pepper

1. Trim broccoli, discarding tough stems. Cut broccoli into florets with 2-inch stems. Peel remaining stems; cut into ½-inch slices.

2. Bring 1 quart water to a boil in large saucepan over medium-high heat. Add broccoli; return to a boil. Cook 3 to 5 minutes or until broccoli is tender. Drain; transfer to serving dish.

3. Combine lemon juice, oil, garlic, parsley, salt and pepper in small bowl. Pour over broccoli; toss to coat. Cover and let stand 1 hour before serving to allow flavors to blend. Serve at room temperature.

Ratatouille with Parmesan Cheese

MAKES 4 SERVINGS

1 baby eggplant, diced *or* 1 cup diced regular eggplant

2 medium tomatoes, chopped

1 small zucchini, diced

1 cup sliced mushrooms

½ cup tomato purée

1 large shallot *or* ½ small onion, chopped

1 clove garlic, minced

¾ teaspoon dried oregano

½ teaspoon salt

⅛ teaspoon dried rosemary

⅛ teaspoon black pepper

2 tablespoons shredded fresh basil

2 teaspoons lemon juice

¼ cup shredded Parmesan cheese

1. Spray large saucepan with nonstick cooking spray; heat over medium-high heat. Add eggplant; cook and stir about 5 minutes until lightly browned. Add tomatoes, zucchini, mushrooms, tomato purée, shallot, garlic, oregano, salt, rosemary and pepper. Bring to a simmer. Reduce heat to low; cook 30 minutes or until vegetables are softened and flavors have blended.

2. Stir in basil and lemon juice. Top each serving with 1 tablespoon Parmesan cheese.

PER SERVING
calories *96*
total fat *2g*
saturated fat *1g*
carbs *17g*
dietary fiber *7g*
protein *7g*

Greek-Style Cucumber Salad

MAKES 4 SERVINGS (½ CUP PER SERVING)

1 medium cucumber, peeled and diced

¼ cup chopped green onions

1 teaspoon minced fresh dill

1 clove garlic, minced

1 cup sour cream

½ teaspoon salt

¼ teaspoon black pepper

⅛ teaspoon ground cumin

Lemon juice (optional)

1. Combine cucumber, green onions, dill and garlic in medium bowl.

2. Combine sour cream, salt, pepper and cumin in small bowl; stir until blended. Add to cucumber mixture; mix well. Sprinkle with lemon juice to taste, if desired.

PER SERVING
calories *116*
total fat *10g*
saturated fat *6g*
carbs *5g*
dietary fiber *1g*
protein *2g*

Greek Salad

SALAD

- 3 medium tomatoes, cut into 8 wedges each
- 1 green bell pepper, cut into 1-inch pieces
- ½ English cucumber (8 to 10 inches), quartered lengthwise and sliced crosswise
- ½ red onion, thinly sliced
- ½ cup pitted kalamata olives
- 1 block (8 ounces) feta cheese, cut into ½-inch cubes

DRESSING

- 6 tablespoons extra virgin olive oil
- 3 tablespoons red wine vinegar
- 1 to 2 cloves garlic, minced
- ¾ teaspoon dried oregano
- ¾ teaspoon salt
- ¼ teaspoon black pepper

1. Combine tomatoes, bell pepper, cucumber, onion and olives in large bowl. Top with feta.

2. For dressing, whisk oil, vinegar, garlic, oregano, salt and black pepper in small bowl until well blended. Pour over salad; stir gently to coat.

PER SERVING

calories *233*
total fat *21g*
saturated fat *6g*
carbs *7g*
dietary fiber *1g*
protein *8g*

Middle Eastern Spinach Salad

¼ cup lemon juice

1 tablespoon extra virgin olive oil

1 tablespoon packed brown sugar

½ teaspoon curry powder

1 pound fresh spinach

½ cup golden raisins

¼ cup minced red onion

¼ cup thin red onion slices

1. For dressing, whisk lemon juice, oil, brown sugar and curry powder in small bowl until blended.

2. Wash spinach well to remove sand and grit; remove stems and bruised leaves. Drain well; pat dry with paper towels. Tear spinach into bite-size pieces.

3. Combine spinach, raisins, minced onion and onion slices in large bowl. Add dressing; toss gently to coat.

PER SERVING
calories *142*
total fat *4g*
saturated fat *1g*
carbs *27g*
dietary fiber *4g*
protein *4g*

Tuna Salad Niçoise

MAKES 6 SERVINGS

HERB VINAIGRETTE

- ¼ cup white wine vinegar
- ¼ cup red wine vinegar
- ¼ cup chopped fresh basil
- 2 tablespoons chopped fresh chives
- 1 tablespoon Dijon mustard
- 2 cloves garlic, minced
- ½ teaspoon sugar
- ½ teaspoon salt
- ½ teaspoon black pepper
  Red pepper flakes (optional)
- 1 cup olive oil

SALAD

- 1 pound tuna steaks*
- 1½ pounds red potatoes, cubed
- 2 cups trimmed and halved green beans
- 8 cups mixed salad greens or chopped romaine lettuce
- 3 hard-cooked eggs, cut into wedges
- ½ cup pitted kalamata or black Niçoise olives
- 4 tomatoes, cut into wedges

Or substitute 2 cans (6 ounces each) tuna, drained and flaked and skip steps 2 and 3.

1. For vinaigrette, place all ingredients except oil in medium bowl; whisk until blended. Gradually whisk in oil in thin steady stream. Pour dressing into jar; refrigerate until ready to use.

2. Place tuna in baking dish. Pour ¼ cup dressing over tuna; turn to coat. Marinate in refrigerator 30 minutes.

3. Prepare grill for direct cooking over medium heat or preheat broiler. Remove tuna from marinade, discarding marinade. Grill or broil tuna 8 minutes or until tuna is desired doneness, turning once. Thinly slice tuna.

4. Bring large saucepan of salted water to a boil. Add potatoes; cook 5 minutes. Add green beans; cook 5 minutes or until potatoes are tender and green beans are crisp-tender. Drain and return to saucepan. Add ¼ cup dressing; stir to coat.

5. Arrange lettuce on serving platter; top with potato and green bean mixture. Arrange eggs, olives, tomatoes and tuna on top. Serve with remaining dressing.

PER SERVING
calories *670*
total fat *52g*
saturated fat *7g*
carbs *27g*
dietary fiber *4g*
protein *24g*

PER SERVING
calories *470*
total fat *14g*
saturated fat *2g*
carbs *66g*
dietary fiber *19g*
protein *22g*

SOUPS
& STEWS

Fasolada
(Greek White Bean Soup)
MAKES 4 SERVINGS

- 4 tablespoons extra virgin olive oil, divided
- 1 large onion, diced
- 3 stalks celery, diced
- 3 carrots, diced
- 4 cloves garlic, minced
- ¼ cup tomato paste
- 1 teaspoon salt
- 1 teaspoon dried oregano

- ½ teaspoon ground cumin
- ¼ teaspoon black pepper
- 1 bay leaf
- 4 cups vegetable broth
- 3 cans (about 15 ounces each) cannellini beans, rinsed and drained
- 2 tablespoons lemon juice
- ¼ cup minced fresh parsley

1. Heat 2 tablespoons oil in large saucepan over medium-high heat. Add onion, celery and carrots; cook and stir 8 to 10 minutes or until vegetables are softened. Stir in garlic; cook and stir 30 seconds. Stir in tomato paste, salt, oregano, cumin, pepper and bay leaf; cook and stir 30 seconds.

2. Stir in broth; bring to a boil. Stir in beans; return to a boil. Reduce heat to medium-low; simmer 30 minutes. Stir in remaining 2 tablespoons oil and lemon juice. Remove and discard bay leaf. Sprinkle with parsley just before serving.

Spinach and Cumin Chicken Soup

MAKES 4 SERVINGS

2½ cups water

1 can (about 14 ounces) chicken broth

1 can (about 15 ounces) chickpeas, rinsed and drained

1 cup chopped cooked chicken

1 small onion, chopped

1 carrot, chopped

1 clove garlic, minced

1 teaspoon dried oregano

1 teaspoon ground cumin

½ (10-ounce) package fresh spinach, stemmed and coarsely chopped *or* 1 bag (5 ounces) baby spinach

⅛ teaspoon black pepper

1. Combine water, broth, chickpeas, chicken, onion, carrot, garlic, oregano and cumin in medium saucepan. Bring to a boil over high heat. Reduce heat to medium-low; cover and simmer 15 minutes.

2. Stir in spinach and pepper; simmer, uncovered, 2 minutes or until spinach is wilted.

Mediterranean Fish Soup

MAKES 4 SERVINGS

4 ounces uncooked mini penne, orzo or other small pasta

¾ cup chopped onion

2 cloves garlic, minced

1 teaspoon whole fennel seeds

1 can (about 14 ounces) stewed tomatoes

1 can (about 14 ounces) chicken broth

1 tablespoon minced fresh parsley

½ teaspoon black pepper

¼ teaspoon salt

¼ teaspoon ground turmeric

8 ounces firm white fish, cut into 1-inch pieces

3 ounces small raw shrimp, peeled (with tails on)

1. Cook pasta in large saucepan of boiling salted water according to package directions for al dente. Drain.

2. Spray large saucepan with nonstick cooking spray; heat over medium heat. Add onion, garlic and fennel seeds; cook and stir 3 minutes or until onion is crisp-tender.

3. Stir in tomatoes, broth, parsley, pepper, salt and turmeric; bring to a boil. Reduce heat to low; simmer 10 minutes.

4. Stir fish into saucepan; cook 1 minute. Add shrimp; cook until shrimp turn pink and opaque. Divide pasta evenly among four bowls; ladle soup evenly over pasta.

Vegetable and Red Lentil Soup

MAKES 4 SERVINGS

1 can (about 14 ounces) vegetable broth

1 can (about 14 ounces) diced tomatoes

2 medium zucchini or yellow summer squash (or 1 of each), chopped

1 red or yellow bell pepper, chopped

½ cup thinly sliced carrots

½ cup dried red lentils, rinsed and sorted

½ teaspoon salt

½ teaspoon sugar

¼ teaspoon black pepper

2 tablespoons chopped fresh basil or thyme

1. Combine broth, tomatoes, zucchini, bell pepper, carrots, lentils, salt, sugar and black pepper in large saucepan. Bring to a simmer over medium-high heat. Reduce heat to medium-low; cover and simmer about 30 minutes or until vegetables and lentils are tender.

2. Ladle into bowls; top with basil.

PER SERVING
calories *147*
total fat *1g*
saturated fat *0g*
carbs *27g*
dietary fiber *10g*
protein *9g*

Middle Eastern Butternut Squash Soup

MAKES 6 SERVINGS

2 teaspoons extra virgin olive oil

1 medium onion, chopped

2 carrots, sliced

1 stalk celery, sliced

2 cloves garlic

1 medium butternut squash (about 2 pounds), peeled, seeded and cubed

3 cups vegetable broth

1 teaspoon ground cinnamon

1 teaspoon green pepper sauce

¾ teaspoon salt

½ teaspoon ground coriander

6 slices French bread, toasted

Chopped fresh parsley

1. Heat oil in large saucepan. Add onion, carrots and celery; cook and stir about 5 minutes or until softened. Add garlic; cook and stir 1 minute.

2. Add squash, broth, cinnamon, pepper sauce, salt and coriander to saucepan. Bring to a boil over high heat. Reduce heat to medium-low; cover and simmer 15 minutes or until squash is tender. Remove from heat.

3. Blend with immersion blender or blend soup in batches in food processor or blender until smooth. Ladle soup into bowls. Top with toast and sprinkle with parsley.

Ribollita (Tuscan Bread Soup)

MAKES 6 SERVINGS

2 tablespoons extra virgin olive oil

1 onion, halved and thinly sliced

2 stalks celery, diced

1 large carrot, julienned or chopped

2 medium zucchini, halved lengthwise and thinly sliced

1 medium yellow squash, halved lengthwise and thinly sliced

3 cloves garlic, minced

1 can (28 ounces) whole tomatoes, undrained

1 can (about 15 ounces) cannellini beans, rinsed and drained

1½ teaspoons salt

1 teaspoon Italian seasoning

¼ teaspoon black pepper

1 bay leaf

¼ teaspoon red pepper flakes (optional)

4 cups vegetable broth

2 cups water

1 bunch kale, stemmed and coarsely chopped *or* 3 cups thinly sliced cabbage

8 ounces Tuscan or other rustic bread, cubed

Shredded Parmesan cheese (optional)

1. Heat oil in large saucepan over medium-high heat. Add onion, celery and carrot; cook and stir 5 minutes. Add zucchini, yellow squash and garlic; cook and stir 5 minutes.

2. Add tomatoes, beans, salt, Italian seasoning, black pepper, bay leaf and red pepper flakes, if desired. Stir in broth and water; bring to a boil. Reduce heat; simmer 15 minutes. Add kale and bread; simmer 10 minutes or until vegetables are tender, bread is soft and soup is thick.

3. Ladle soup into bowls; top with Parmesan cheese, if desired.

PER SERVING
calories *290*
total fat *8g*
saturated fat *2g*
carbs *45g*
dietary fiber *3g*
protein *11g*

Lentil Soup

MAKES 4 SERVINGS

2 tablespoons extra virgin olive oil

1 onion, chopped

1 red bell pepper, chopped

1 teaspoon whole fennel seeds

½ teaspoon ground cumin

¼ teaspoon ground red pepper

4 cups water

1 cup dried lentils, rinsed and sorted

½ teaspoon salt

1 tablespoon lemon juice

½ cup plain 2% or nonfat Greek yogurt

2 tablespoons chopped fresh parsley

1. Heat oil in large saucepan over medium-high heat. Add onion and bell pepper; cook and stir 5 minutes or until tender. Add fennel seeds, cumin and red pepper; cook and stir 1 minute.

2. Add water, lentils and salt; bring to a boil. Reduce heat to low; cover and simmer 25 to 30 minutes or until lentils are tender. Stir in lemon juice.

3. Top each serving with yogurt; sprinkle with parsley.

NOTE: Sometimes packages of lentils may contain small stones or other foreign matter. Place the lentils in a fine-mesh strainer and rinse them under cold water, sorting through and picking out any debris.

PER SERVING
calories *266*
total fat *8g*
saturated fat *1g*
carbs *35g*
dietary fiber *16g*
protein *16g*

Corn and Crab Gazpacho

MAKES 6 SERVINGS

1 cucumber, peeled, seeded and coarsely chopped

3 green onions, coarsely chopped

2 tablespoons coarsely chopped fresh parsley or cilantro

2 pounds grape or cherry tomatoes

1 cup fresh corn, cooked if desired *or* 1 cup thawed frozen corn

3 cups tomato juice, chilled

3 tablespoons extra virgin olive oil

2 tablespoons red wine vinegar

1¼ teaspoons red pepper flakes

1 teaspoon salt

¼ teaspoon black pepper

1½ cups flaked cooked crabmeat (about 8 ounces) *or* 8 ounces cooked baby shrimp

1. Combine cucumber, green onions and parsley in food processor. Process using on/off pulses until finely chopped. Transfer to large pitcher or bowl. Add tomatoes to food processor. Process using on/off pulses until finely chopped. Add to cucumber mixture.

2. Stir corn into pitcher. Add tomato juice, oil, vinegar, red pepper flakes, salt and black pepper. Stir well. Cover; refrigerate 1 to 3 hours.

3. Pour gazpacho into six bowls. Top each serving with ¼ cup crabmeat.

PER SERVING
calories *200*
total fat *8g*
saturated fat *1g*
carbs *23g*
dietary fiber *4g*
protein *10g*

Moroccan Lentil and Vegetable Soup

MAKES 6 SERVINGS

1 tablespoon extra virgin olive oil

1 cup chopped onion

½ cup chopped celery

4 cloves garlic, minced

½ cup dried lentils, rinsed and sorted

1½ teaspoons ground coriander

1½ teaspoons ground cumin

½ teaspoon salt

½ teaspoon ground cinnamon

½ teaspoon black pepper

4 cups vegetable broth

½ cup chopped sun-dried tomatoes (not packed in oil)

1 yellow squash, chopped

½ cup chopped green bell pepper

1 cup chopped plum tomatoes

½ cup chopped fresh parsley

¼ cup chopped fresh cilantro or basil

1. Heat oil in medium saucepan over medium-high heat. Add onion, celery and garlic; cook and stir 5 minutes or until onion is tender. Stir in lentils, coriander, cumin, salt, cinnamon and black pepper; cook 2 minutes. Add broth and sun-dried tomatoes; bring to a boil. Reduce heat to medium-low; cover and simmer 25 minutes.

2. Stir in squash and bell pepper; cover and cook 10 minutes or until lentils are tender.

3. Ladle into bowls. Top with plum tomatoes, parsley and cilantro just before serving.

TIP: Many soups, including this one, taste even better the next day after the flavors have had time to blend. Cover and refrigerate the soup overnight, reserving the plum tomatoes, parsley and cilantro until ready to serve.

Vichyssoise

¼ cup (½ stick) butter

4 medium leeks, sliced
   (white part only)

1 medium onion, sliced

2 pounds potatoes, thinly sliced
   (about 6 medium)

4 cups vegetable broth

2½ cups milk

2 cups half-and-half

Salt

Chopped fresh chives
   (optional)

1. Melt butter in large saucepan over medium heat. Add leeks and onion; cook and stir 5 minutes. Add potatoes and broth. Bring to a boil. Reduce heat; simmer 30 minutes or until potatoes are very tender.

2. Blend with immersion blender or blend soup in batches in food processor or blender until smooth. Return mixture to saucepan.

3. Stir in milk; bring to a boil. Remove from heat; cool 20 minutes. Strain soup through fine-mesh strainer into large bowl or pitcher. Stir in half-and-half; season to taste with salt. Refrigerate until chilled. Spoon soup into chilled bowls or cups. Sprinkle with chives, if desired.

PER SERVING
calories *270*
total fat *11g*
saturated fat *7g*
carbs *34g*
dietary fiber *3g*
protein *8g*

Mediterranean Vegetable Stew

MAKES 6 SERVINGS

8 ounces fresh okra *or* 1 package (10 ounces) frozen cut okra, thawed

1 tablespoon extra virgin olive oil

1½ cups chopped onions

1 clove garlic, minced

1 teaspoon salt

½ teaspoon ground cumin

½ teaspoon ground turmeric

¼ teaspoon ground cinnamon

¼ teaspoon ground red pepper

¼ teaspoon paprika

1 medium butternut squash, peeled, seeded and cut into 1-inch cubes

2 cups cubed unpeeled eggplant

2 cups sliced zucchini

1 medium carrot, sliced

1 can (8 ounces) tomato sauce

½ cup vegetable broth or water

1 can (about 15 ounces) chickpeas, rinsed and drained

1 medium tomato, chopped

⅓ cup raisins

6 cups hot cooked couscous

Minced fresh parsley

1. Wash okra under cold running water. Cut into ¾-inch slices.

2. Heat oil in large saucepan over high heat. Add onions and garlic; cook and stir 5 minutes or until tender. Stir in salt, cumin, turmeric, cinnamon, red pepper and paprika; cook and stir 2 minutes.

3. Add okra, squash, eggplant, zucchini, carrot, tomato sauce and broth. Bring to a boil over high heat. Reduce heat to low. Simmer, uncovered, 5 minutes.

4. Add chickpeas, tomato and raisins; cover and simmer 30 minutes. Serve over couscous; sprinkle with parsley.

PER SERVING
calories *422*
total fat *4g*
saturated fat *1g*
carbs *85g*
dietary fiber *12g*
protein *14g*

GRAINS
& BEANS

Asparagus Barley Risotto

MAKES 4 SERVINGS

- 2 tablespoons extra virgin olive oil
- 1 cup chopped onion
- 1 clove garlic, minced
- 1 teaspoon salt
- ¼ teaspoon black pepper
- ⅛ teaspoon dried marjoram
- 1 cup uncooked pearl barley
- ¼ cup dry white wine
- 3 cups vegetable broth
- 2 cups cut asparagus (1-inch pieces)
- ¼ cup shredded Parmesan cheese

1. Heat oil in medium saucepan over medium heat. Add onion; cook and stir 5 minutes or until softened. Add garlic, salt, pepper and marjoram; cook and stir 1 minute. Add barley; cook and stir 3 minutes or until toasted. Add wine; cook 1 minute or until wine has evaporated, stirring constantly. Add broth; bring to a boil. Reduce heat; cover and simmer 20 minutes or until barley is just tender, stirring occasionally.

2. Stir in asparagus; cover and cook until asparagus is tender and liquid is absorbed. Sprinkle with cheese just before serving.

Vegetable Risotto

MAKES 4 SERVINGS

4 cups vegetable broth

2 tablespoons extra virgin olive oil, divided

1 medium zucchini, cubed

1 medium yellow squash, cubed

1 cup chopped onion

1 cup sliced stemmed shiitake or cremini mushrooms

1 clove garlic, minced

3 plum tomatoes, seeded and chopped

1 teaspoon dried oregano

1 cup uncooked arborio rice

½ teaspoon salt

¼ teaspoon black pepper

¼ cup grated Parmesan cheese

½ cup frozen peas, thawed

1. Bring broth to a simmer in medium saucepan.

2. Heat 1 tablespoon oil in large saucepan or Dutch oven over medium heat. Add zucchini and yellow squash; cook and stir 5 minutes or until crisp-tender. Transfer to medium bowl.

3. Add onion, mushrooms and garlic to large saucepan; cook and stir 5 minutes or until tender. Add tomatoes and oregano; cook and stir 2 to 3 minutes or until tomatoes are softened. Transfer to bowl with zucchini mixture.

4. Heat remaining 1 tablespoon oil in same saucepan over medium heat. Add rice; cook and stir 2 minutes. Stir in salt and pepper.

5. Add about ¾ cup broth to rice; cook and stir until broth is absorbed. Repeat with remaining broth. Cook until rice is tender, but still firm. (Total cooking time will be 20 to 25 minutes.)

6. Stir in cheese, reserved vegetables and peas; cook until heated through. Taste and adjust seasonings. Serve immediately.

calories *394*
total fat *9g*
saturated fat *2g*
carbs *56g*
dietary fiber *5g*
protein *10g*

Spiced Chickpeas and Couscous

1 can (about 14 ounces) vegetable broth

1 teaspoon ground coriander

½ teaspoon ground cardamom

½ teaspoon ground turmeric

½ teaspoon hot pepper sauce

¼ teaspoon salt

⅛ teaspoon ground cinnamon

1 cup julienned or shredded carrots

1 can (about 15 ounces) chickpeas, rinsed and drained

1 cup frozen peas

1 cup couscous

2 tablespoons chopped fresh mint or parsley

1. Combine broth, coriander, cardamom, turmeric, hot pepper sauce, salt and cinnamon in large saucepan; bring to a boil over high heat. Add carrots; reduce heat and simmer 5 minutes.

2. Add chickpeas and frozen peas; return to a simmer. Simmer, uncovered, 2 minutes.

3. Stir in couscous. Remove from heat; cover and let stand 5 minutes or until liquid is absorbed. Sprinkle with mint.

PER SERVING
calories *226*
total fat *2g*
saturated fat *1g*
carbs *44g*
dietary fiber *10g*
protein *9g*

Bulgur Pilaf with Tomato and Zucchini

MAKES 8 SERVINGS

1 cup uncooked bulgur wheat

1 tablespoon extra virgin olive oil

¾ cup chopped onion

2 cloves garlic, minced

1 can (about 14 ounces) whole tomatoes, drained and coarsely chopped

2 small zucchini (8 ounces), thinly sliced

1 cup vegetable broth

1 teaspoon dried basil

½ teaspoon salt

⅛ teaspoon black pepper

1. Place bulgur in fine-mesh strainer. Rinse well under cold water, removing any debris. Drain; set aside.

2. Heat oil in large saucepan over medium heat. Add onion and garlic; cook and stir 5 minutes or until onion is softened. Stir in tomatoes and zucchini; reduce heat to medium-low. Cover and cook 15 minutes or until zucchini is almost tender, stirring occasionally.

3. Stir bulgur, broth, basil, salt and pepper into vegetable mixture. Bring to a boil over high heat. Remove from heat. Cover and let stand 10 minutes or until liquid is absorbed. Stir gently before serving.

PER SERVING
calories *120*
total fat *2g*
saturated fat *0g*
carbs *21g*
dietary fiber *5g*
protein *4g*

Italian Eggplant with Millet and Pepper Stuffing

MAKES 4 SERVINGS

¼ cup uncooked millet

2 small eggplants (about 6 ounces each)

¼ cup chopped red bell pepper, divided

¼ cup chopped green bell pepper, divided

1 teaspoon extra virgin olive oil

1 clove garlic, minced

1½ cups vegetable broth

½ teaspoon ground cumin

½ teaspoon dried oregano

¼ teaspoon salt

⅛ teaspoon red pepper flakes

1. Cook and stir millet in large heavy skillet over medium heat 5 minutes or until golden. Transfer to small bowl; set aside.

2. Slice eggplants in half lengthwise. Scoop out flesh, leaving ¼-inch shell. Finely chop scooped out flesh. Combine 1 tablespoon red bell pepper and 1 tablespoon green bell pepper in small bowl; set aside.

3. Heat oil in same skillet over medium heat. Add chopped eggplant, remaining red and green bell pepper and garlic; cook and stir about 8 minutes or until eggplant is tender.

4. Stir in toasted millet, broth, cumin, oregano, salt and red pepper flakes. Bring to a boil over high heat. Reduce heat to medium-low. Cover and cook 35 minutes or until all liquid is absorbed and millet is tender. Remove from heat; let stand, covered, 10 minutes.

5. Preheat oven to 350°F. Pour 1 cup water into 8-inch square baking pan. Fill eggplant shells with millet mixture. Sprinkle with reserved chopped bell peppers, pressing in lightly. Carefully place filled shells in prepared pan. Bake 15 minutes or until heated through.

PER SERVING
calories *89*
total fat *2g*
saturated fat *1g*
carbs *17g*
dietary fiber *5g*
protein *3g*

Mujadara
MAKES 6 SERVINGS

1 cup dried lentils, rinsed and sorted

¼ cup plus 1 tablespoon extra virgin olive oil, divided

3 sweet onions, thinly sliced

2½ teaspoons salt, divided

1½ teaspoons ground cumin

1 teaspoon ground allspice

1 cinnamon stick

1 bay leaf

⅛ to ¼ teaspoon ground red pepper

¾ cup uncooked long grain rice, rinsed and drained

3 cups vegetable broth or water

1 cucumber

1 cup plain Greek yogurt or sour cream

1. Place lentils in medium saucepan; cover with water by 1 inch. Bring to a boil over medium-high heat. Reduce heat to medium-low; simmer 10 minutes. Drain and rinse under cold water.

2. Meanwhile, heat ¼ cup oil in large saucepan or Dutch oven. Add onions and 1 teaspoon salt; cook and stir 15 minutes or until golden and parts are crispy. Remove most of onions to small bowl, leaving about ½ cup in saucepan.*

3. Add remaining 1 tablespoon oil to saucepan with onions; heat over medium-high heat. Add cumin, allspice, cinnamon stick, bay leaf and red pepper; cook and stir 30 seconds. Add rice; cook and stir 2 to 3 minutes or until rice is lightly toasted. Add broth, lentils and 1 teaspoon salt; bring to a boil. Reduce heat to low; cover and cook about 15 minutes or until broth is absorbed and rice and lentils are tender. Remove saucepan from heat. Place clean kitchen towel over top of saucepan; replace lid and let stand 5 to 10 minutes.

4. Meanwhile, peel cucumber and trim ends. Grate cucumber on large holes of box grater; squeeze out excess liquid. Place in medium bowl; stir in yogurt and remaining ½ teaspoon salt. Serve lentils and rice with reserved onions and cucumber sauce.

If desired, continue to cook reserved onions in additional oil in a medium skillet over medium heat until dark golden brown.

Greek Giant Beans in Tomato Sauce

MAKES 8 SERVINGS (1 CUP EACH)

1 pound dried gigante beans*
  (about 2¼ cups)

2 bay leaves

1½ tablespoons salt, divided

¼ cup extra virgin olive oil

2 small onions, chopped

1 stalk celery, finely chopped

1 medium carrot, finely chopped

3 cloves garlic, minced

2 tablespoons tomato paste

1 teaspoon dried oregano, plus
  additional for serving

½ teaspoon black pepper

⅛ teaspoon red pepper flakes

1 can (28 ounces) whole
  tomatoes, undrained,
  coarsely chopped or
  crushed with hands**

Chopped fresh parsley

Crumbled feta cheese

*If gigante beans are not available,
use another variety of large white
bean such as lima, butter or corona
beans.

**Or substitute 1 can (28 ounces)
diced tomatoes.

1. Combine beans, 6 cups water, bay leaves and 1 tablespoon salt in large saucepan. Bring to a boil over high heat. Reduce heat to medium-low; simmer 1 hour or until beans are tender enough to bite but not completely cooked.

2. Meanwhile, heat oil in medium saucepan over medium-high heat. Add onions, celery, carrot and garlic; cook and stir 8 minutes or until vegetables are tender. Add tomato paste, 1½ teaspoons salt, 1 teaspoon oregano, black pepper and red pepper flakes; cook and stir 1 minute. Stir in tomatoes; remove from heat.

3. Preheat oven to 350°F. Drain beans, discarding bay leaves and any loose bean skins, reserving 2 cups cooking water. Combine beans, reserved water and tomato sauce in large bowl. Spread in 13×9-inch baking dish. Bake about 2 hours or until beans are tender and creamy, stirring every 30 minutes.

4. Sprinkle with parsley, cheese and additional oregano.

Easy Oven Polenta
with Mushroom Sauce
MAKES 6 SERVINGS

POLENTA

  5 cups water
  1 tablespoon sugar
  1 teaspoon salt
  1 cup yellow cornmeal
  ½ cup grated Parmesan or
     Romano cheese

MUSHROOM SAUCE

  2 tablespoons extra virgin
     olive oil
  1 large red onion, chopped
  2 pounds button or cremini
     mushrooms, thickly sliced
  ½ teaspoon salt
  ½ teaspoon dried thyme
  ½ teaspoon dried sage
  ½ teaspoon black pepper
  1 teaspoon minced garlic
  1 tablespoon all-purpose flour
  1 cup dry white wine or water

1. Preheat oven to 350°F.

2. For polenta, combine water, sugar and 1 teaspoon salt in large ovenproof saucepan. Bring to a boil over medium-high heat. Gradually whisk in cornmeal; reduce heat to low. Cook 5 minutes or until thickened, stirring often. Cover with tight-fitting lid; bake 1 hour. Stir in cheese.

3. Meanwhile for mushroom sauce, heat oil in large skillet over medium-high heat. Add onion; cook and stir 5 minutes or until softened. Add mushrooms; cook and stir until browned. Stir in ½ teaspoon salt, thyme, sage and pepper; cook 1 minute. Stir in garlic; cook 1 minute. Sprinkle flour over mixture; cook 1 minute, stirring constantly. Add wine; cook and stir until sauce thickens. Reduce heat to low. Cover; simmer 15 minutes, stirring occasionally.

4. Divide polenta among six bowls; top with mushroom sauce.

Spanish-Style Paella

MAKES 8 SERVINGS

6 cups chicken broth

3 tablespoons extra virgin olive oil

½ pound boneless skinless chicken thighs, cut into bite-size pieces

2 to 3 links chorizo sausage (about 5 ounces), sliced

1 medium onion, chopped

1 red bell pepper, chopped

4 cloves garlic, minced

1 teaspoon saffron threads, lightly crushed

1½ cups uncooked long grain rice

1 can (10 ounces) diced tomatoes with chiles

3 tablespoons tomato paste

½ teaspoon salt

¼ teaspoon black pepper

1 pound large raw shrimp, peeled and deveined (with tails on)

½ pound mussels, scrubbed and debearded

½ cup frozen peas, thawed

1. Bring broth to a boil in medium saucepan. Reduce heat to low; keep warm.

2. Heat oil in cast iron skillet over medium-high heat. Add chicken and chorizo; cook 1 minute, stirring once. Add onion, bell pepper, garlic and saffron; cook and stir 5 minutes or until vegetables are softened and chorizo is browned.

3. Add rice, tomatoes, tomato paste, salt and black pepper; cook 5 minutes, stirring occasionally. Add broth about 1 cup at a time, stirring after each addition until broth is almost absorbed.

4. Cover skillet with foil; cook over medium heat 25 to 30 minutes or until rice is tender. Remove foil; gently stir in shrimp, mussels and peas. Replace foil; cook 5 to 10 minutes or until shrimp are pink and opaque and mussels open. Discard any unopened mussels.

Mushroom and Romano Risotto

MAKES 4 SERVINGS

4½ cups vegetable broth

3 tablespoons extra virgin olive oil

8 ounces sliced mushrooms

½ cup chopped shallots

½ cup chopped onion

3 cloves garlic, minced

1½ cups uncooked arborio rice

1 teaspoon salt

½ cup Madeira wine

½ cup grated Romano cheese

3 tablespoons butter, softened

3 tablespoons chopped fresh parsley

¼ teaspoon black pepper

1. Bring broth to a simmer in medium saucepan.

2. Heat oil in large saucepan or Dutch oven over medium-high heat. Add mushrooms; cook and stir 6 to 7 minutes or until beginning to brown. Stir in shallots, onion and garlic; cook and stir 2 to 3 minutes or until vegetables begin to soften. Add rice and salt; cook and stir 1 minute. Add Madeira; cook and stir 1 minute or until almost absorbed.

3. Add about ¾ cup broth to rice; cook and stir until broth is absorbed. Repeat with remaining broth. Cook until rice is tender, but still firm. (Total cooking time will be 20 to 25 minutes.)

4. Remove from heat; stir in cheese, butter, parsley and pepper. Serve immediately.

Greek Rice

MAKES 6 SERVINGS

2 tablespoons butter

1¾ cups uncooked long grain rice

2 cans (about 14 ounces each) vegetable broth

1 teaspoon Greek seasoning

1 teaspoon dried oregano

½ teaspoon salt

1 cup pitted kalamata olives, drained and chopped

¾ cup chopped roasted red peppers

Crumbled feta cheese (optional)

Chopped fresh parsley (optional)

1. Melt butter in large nonstick skillet over medium heat. Add rice; cook and stir 4 minutes or until golden brown. Add broth, Greek seasoning, oregano and salt; bring to a boil. Reduce heat to low; cover and simmer about 15 minutes or until broth is absorbed and rice is tender. Remove from heat; let stand, covered, 5 minutes.

2. Stir in olives and roasted red peppers. Top with cheese and parsley, if desired.

PASTA
& COUSCOUS

Pasta e Ceci
MAKES 4 SERVINGS

4 tablespoons extra virgin
  olive oil, divided

1 onion, chopped

1 carrot, chopped

1 clove garlic, minced

1 sprig fresh rosemary

1 teaspoon salt

1 can (28 ounces) whole
  tomatoes, drained and
  crushed (see Note)

2 cups vegetable broth

1 can (about 15 ounces)
  chickpeas, undrained

1 bay leaf

⅛ teaspoon red pepper flakes

1 cup uncooked orecchiette
  pasta

Black pepper

Chopped fresh parsley or basil
  (optional)

1. Heat 3 tablespoons oil in large saucepan over medium-high heat. Add onion and carrot; cook 10 minutes or until vegetables are softened, stirring occasionally.

2. Add garlic, rosemary and salt; cook and stir 1 minute. Stir in tomatoes, broth, chickpeas with liquid, bay leaf and red pepper flakes. Remove 1 cup mixture to food processor or blender; process until smooth. Stir back into saucepan; bring to a boil.

3. Stir in pasta. Reduce heat to medium; cook 12 to 15 minutes or until pasta is tender and mixture is creamy. Remove and discard bay leaf and rosemary sprig. Stir in black pepper; taste and adjust seasonings. Divide among four bowls; sprinkle with parsley, if desired, and drizzle with remaining 1 tablespoon oil.

NOTE: To crush the tomatoes, take them out of the can one at a time and crush them between your fingers over the pot. Or coarsely chop them with a knife.

Lentils with Pasta

MAKES 6 SERVINGS

1 cup dried lentils

1 cup dried split peas

1 tablespoon extra virgin olive oil

1 onion, chopped

2 tablespoons tomato paste

2 cloves garlic, minced

1 teaspoon salt

¼ teaspoon black pepper

1 can (about 14 ounces) diced tomatoes

3 cups water

12 ounces uncooked short pasta (small shells, elbow macaroni, ditalini or similar)

Shredded Romano or Parmesan cheese (optional)

1. Place lentils and split peas in medium bowl; cover with water. Let stand at least 10 minutes.

2. Heat oil in large saucepan or Dutch oven over medium heat. Add onion; cook and stir 6 to 8 minutes or until onion is lightly browned. Add tomato paste, garlic, salt and pepper; cook and stir 1 minute. Add tomatoes and 3 cups water; bring to a boil.

3. Drain lentils and split peas and add to saucepan. Reduce heat to medium-low; cover and simmer about 40 minutes or until lentils and split peas are tender.

4. Meanwhile, cook pasta in large saucepan of salted boiling water according to package directions for al dente. Drain and add to lentil mixture; mix well. Serve with cheese, if desired.

PER SERVING
calories *490*
total fat *4g*
saturated fat *0g*
carbs *90g*
dietary fiber *14g*
protein *24g*

Pasta with Roasted Tomatoes and Feta

MAKES 6 SERVINGS

- 2 pints grape and/or cherry tomatoes
- 4 cloves garlic, crushed and peeled, divided
- ¼ cup extra virgin olive oil
- ½ teaspoon salt
- ¼ teaspoon black pepper
- 1 block (8 ounces) feta cheese
- 8 ounces uncooked rotini, cellentani or spaghetti

1. Preheat oven to 400°F. Combine tomatoes, 3 cloves garlic, oil, salt and pepper. Transfer to 13×9-inch baking dish. Place cheese in middle of baking dish, not resting on tomatoes.

2. Bake 30 minutes. *Increase oven temperature to 450°F;* bake 15 minutes or until tomatoes are very soft and cheese is browned around edges.

3. Meanwhile, cook pasta in large saucepan of salted boiling water until al dente. Drain, reserving 1 cup cooking water.

4. Scrape tomato mixture into large bowl. Add pasta; mix until well blended, adding enough cooking water until sauce is creamy and pasta is coated.

Couscous and Apricots

MAKES 4 SERVINGS

1 can (5½ ounces) apricot nectar
    or apple juice

½ cup thinly sliced celery

½ cup water

¼ cup chopped dried apricots

½ teaspoon salt

¼ teaspoon ground allspice

⅓ cup uncooked couscous

⅓ cup uncooked quick-cooking
    brown rice

¼ cup coarsely chopped walnuts

1. Combine apricot nectar, celery, water, apricots, salt and allspice in large saucepan. Bring to a boil over high heat. Remove from heat. Stir in couscous, brown rice and walnuts. Cover; let stand 5 minutes or until liquid is absorbed.

2. Fluff couscous mixture with fork.

PER SERVING
calories *206*
total fat *5g*
saturated fat *1g*
carbs *36g*
dietary fiber *5g*
protein *6g*

Artichoke Pasta

MAKES 4 SERVINGS

1 tablespoon extra virgin olive oil

1 cup chopped sweet onion

4 cloves garlic, minced

1 can (28 ounces) crushed tomatoes

1 can (about 14 ounces) artichoke hearts, drained and cut into pieces

1 cup small pimiento-stuffed olives

¾ teaspoon red pepper flakes

8 ounces uncooked fettuccine

½ cup shredded Asiago or Romano cheese

Torn fresh basil leaves (optional)

1. Heat oil in large saucepan over medium heat. Add onion; cook and stir 5 minutes or until softened. Add garlic; cook and stir 1 minute. Stir in tomatoes, artichokes, olives and red pepper flakes. Bring to a simmer. Reduce heat to medium-low; cover and cook 45 minutes.

2. Cook pasta in large saucepan of salted boiling water according to package directions for al dente. Drain; divide among serving bowls. Top with sauce, cheese and basil, if desired.

Orzo with Spinach and Red Pepper

MAKES 6 SERVINGS

4 ounces uncooked orzo pasta

1 teaspoon extra virgin olive oil

1 medium red bell pepper, diced

3 cloves garlic, minced

1 package (10 ounces) frozen chopped spinach, thawed and squeezed dry

¼ cup grated Parmesan cheese

1 teaspoon finely chopped fresh oregano or basil (optional)

¼ teaspoon lemon pepper

1. Cook orzo in medium saucepan of salted boiling water according to package directions for al dente. Drain; set aside.

2. Heat oil in large skillet over medium-high heat. Add bell pepper and garlic; cook and stir 3 minutes or until bell pepper is crisp-tender. Add orzo and spinach; cook and stir until heated through. Remove from heat.

3. Stir in cheese, oregano, if desired, and lemon pepper.

Easy Slow Cooker Ziti Ratatouille

MAKES 6 SERVINGS

1 large eggplant, peeled and cut into ½-inch cubes (about 1½ pounds)

2 medium zucchini, cut into ½-inch cubes

1 green or red bell pepper, cut into ½-inch pieces

1 onion, chopped

4 cloves garlic, minced

1 jar (about 24 ounces) marinara sauce

2 cans (about 14 ounces each) diced tomatoes with garlic and onions

8 ounces uncooked ziti pasta

1 can (6 ounces) pitted black olives, drained

Juice of ½ lemon (optional)

Shaved Parmesan cheese (optional)

1. Layer eggplant, zucchini, bell pepper, onion, garlic, marinara sauce and tomatoes in slow cooker. Cover; cook on LOW 4½ hours.

2. Stir in pasta and olives. Cover; cook on LOW 25 minutes or until pasta is tender. Drizzle with lemon juice and sprinkle with Parmesan cheese, if desired.

PER SERVING

calories *275*
total fat *7g*
saturated fat *1g*
carbs *47g*
dietary fiber *7g*
protein *8g*

Grilled Veggies and Couscous
MAKES 6 SERVINGS (1 CUP EACH)

⅓ cup pine nuts

1½ cups vegetable broth or water

2 tablespoons extra virgin olive oil

½ teaspoon salt

1 cup uncooked couscous

1 medium zucchini, cut lengthwise into ½-inch slices

½ small red onion, sliced

1 medium red bell pepper, cut in half

¼ cup crumbled plain or tomato-basil flavored feta cheese

1 clove garlic, minced

Salt and black pepper

½ teaspoon lemon pepper

1. Place pine nuts in small skillet; cook and stir over medium heat 5 minutes or just until lightly browned and fragrant. Transfer to plate to cool.

2. Combine broth, 1 tablespoon oil and ½ teaspoon salt in small saucepan; bring to a boil over medium-high heat. Stir in couscous. Remove from heat; cover and set aside.

3. Prepare grill for direct cooking. Brush vegetables with remaining 1 tablespoon oil. Place vegetables on grid over medium-high heat. Grill zucchini and onion 5 minutes until tender. Grill bell pepper 7 to 10 minutes or until skin is blackened. Place pepper in small plastic bag; seal and set aside 3 to 5 minutes. Remove from bag; scrape off blackened skin. Chop vegetables.

4. Spoon couscous into serving bowl; fluff with fork. Add vegetables, pine nuts, cheese and garlic; season with salt and black pepper. Sprinkle with lemon pepper.

PER SERVING
calories *220*
total fat *10g*
saturated fat *2g*
carbs *27g*
dietary fiber *3g*
protein *6g*

Spaghetti Mediterranean

MAKES 4 SERVINGS

1½ pounds fresh tomatoes (about 4 large)	4 flat anchovy fillets, chopped
8 ounces uncooked spaghetti	1 tablespoon drained capers
¼ cup extra virgin olive oil	1 tablespoon chopped fresh basil *or* ½ teaspoon dried basil
2 cloves garlic, minced	½ teaspoon dried oregano
½ cup chopped fresh parsley	½ teaspoon salt
12 pitted green olives, sliced	¼ teaspoon red pepper flakes

1. Bring large saucepan of water to a boil. Add tomatoes; cook 60 seconds to loosen skins. Immediately drain tomatoes and rinse under cold running water. Peel, seed and coarsely chop tomatoes.

2. Cook spaghetti in large saucepan of salted boiling water according to package directions for al dente. Drain and return to saucepan; keep warm.

3. Meanwhile, heat oil in medium skillet over medium-high heat. Add garlic; cook 45 seconds or just until garlic begins to color. Stir in tomatoes, parsley, olives, anchovies, capers, basil, oregano, salt and red pepper flakes; cook and stir 10 minutes or until most of the liquid has evaporated and sauce is slightly thickened. Pour sauce over spaghetti; toss lightly. Serve immediately.

PER SERVING
calories *400*
total fat *18g*
saturated fat *3g*
carbs *51g*
dietary fiber *5g*
protein *11g*

Tomato, Orzo and Feta Bake

1 package (16 ounces) uncooked
 orzo pasta

1 can (about 14 ounces) diced
 Italian-style tomatoes

1 can (4¼ ounces) chopped black
 olives, drained

2 tablespoons extra virgin
 olive oil

2 cloves garlic, minced

1 teaspoon salt

¼ teaspoon black pepper

1 can (about 14 ounces)
 vegetable broth

6 ounces feta cheese, cut into
 ½-inch cubes

1. Preheat oven to 450°F. Spray 2-quart baking dish with nonstick cooking spray.

2. Combine orzo, tomatoes, olives, oil, garlic, salt and pepper in medium bowl; place
 in prepared baking dish. Add broth; mix well. Top with cheese. Cover with foil.

3. Bake 22 to 24 minutes or until pasta is tender. Remove from oven; let stand
 5 minutes before serving.

PER SERVING
calories *440*
total fat *15g*
saturated fat *5g*
carbs *63g*
dietary fiber *1g*
protein *15g*

Pasta and Potatoes with Pesto

MAKES 6 SERVINGS

- 1 cup tightly packed fresh basil leaves
- 2 tablespoons pine nuts or almonds
- 2 cloves garlic
- ½ teaspoon salt
- ¼ cup plus 1 tablespoon extra virgin olive oil
- ½ cup plus 2 tablespoons grated Parmesan cheese, divided

- 1½ tablespoons grated Romano cheese
- 3 medium unpeeled red potatoes, cut into 1-inch pieces
- 8 ounces uncooked linguine
- ¾ cup frozen peas
- ¼ teaspoon black pepper

1. For pesto, place basil, pine nuts, garlic and ½ teaspoon salt in food processor or blender. With motor running, add oil through feed tube in thin, steady stream; process until well blended and pine nuts are finely chopped. Transfer basil mixture to small bowl; stir in ¼ cup Parmesan cheese and Romano cheese.

2. Bring medium saucepan of salted water to a boil. Add potatoes; cook 10 minutes or until fork-tender. Drain.

3. Meanwhile, cook linguine in large saucepan of salted boiling water according to package directions for al dente, adding peas during last 3 minutes of cooking. Drain, reserving ½ cup pasta water, and return pasta to saucepan. Stir in pesto until well blended, adding some of pasta water if necessary until pasta is coated. Stir in potatoes, ¼ cup Parmesan cheese and pepper.

4. Divide pasta mixture among six plates; sprinkle with remaining 2 tablespoons Parmesan cheese.

PER SERVING
calories *410*
total fat *19g*
saturated fat *5g*
carbs *48g*
dietary fiber *3g*
protein *14g*

Mediterranean Veggies with Navy Bean Penne

MAKES 4 SERVINGS

8 ounces uncooked multigrain or whole wheat penne pasta

1 can (about 15 ounces) navy beans, rinsed and drained

4 teaspoons extra virgin olive oil, divided

1 green bell pepper, chopped

1 large zucchini, thinly sliced

2 cloves garlic, minced

1 can (about 28 ounces) stewed tomatoes

2 teaspoons dried basil

Salt and black pepper

½ cup (2 ounces) shredded mozzarella cheese

2 tablespoons grated Parmesan cheese

1. Cook pasta in large saucepan of boiling salted water according to package directions for al dente, adding beans during last minute of cooking. Drain and return to saucepan; keep warm.

2. Meanwhile, heat 2 teaspoons oil in large skillet over medium-high heat. Add bell pepper and zucchini; cook and stir 5 minutes or until edges are beginning to brown. Add garlic; cook 15 seconds, stirring constantly. Add tomatoes and basil; bring to a boil. Reduce heat to low; cover and simmer 10 minutes.

3. Stir in remaining 2 teaspoons oil. Season with salt and black pepper. Spoon tomato mixture over pasta mixture; sprinkle with mozzarella and Parmesan cheeses.

PER SERVING
calories *520*
total fat *13g*
saturated fat *4g*
carbs *79g*
dietary fiber *10g*
protein *24g*

PER SERVING
calories *350*
total fat *11g*
saturated fat *4g*
carbs *27g*
dietary fiber *9g*
protein *32g*

POULTRY & FISH

Chicken Cassoulet

MAKES 6 SERVINGS

4 slices bacon

¼ cup all-purpose flour

Salt and black pepper

1¾ pounds bone-in chicken pieces

2 chicken sausages (2¼ ounces each), cooked and cut into ¼-inch pieces

1 medium onion, chopped

1½ cups diced red and green bell peppers

2 cloves garlic, minced

1 teaspoon dried thyme

1 teaspoon extra virgin olive oil

½ cup dry white wine

2 cans (about 15 ounces each) cannellini or Great Northern beans, rinsed and drained

1. Preheat oven to 350°F.

2. Cook bacon in Dutch oven over medium-high heat until crisp; drain on paper towels. Cut into 1-inch pieces. Reserve bacon drippings in Dutch oven.

3. Place flour in shallow bowl; season with salt and black pepper. Dip chicken pieces in flour mixture; shake off excess. Heat drippings in Dutch oven over medium-high heat. Cook chicken in batches until browned on all sides. Transfer to plate. Add sausage; cook until lightly browned. Transfer to plate with chicken.

4. Add onion, bell peppers, garlic and thyme to Dutch oven; cook and stir over medium heat 5 minutes or until softened, adding oil as needed to prevent sticking. Add wine, stirring to scrape up browned bits. Add beans; mix well. Top with chicken, sausages and bacon.

5. Cover and bake 40 minutes. Uncover; bake 15 minutes or until chicken is cooked through (165°F).

Broiled Salmon with Cucumber Yogurt

MAKES 4 SERVINGS

1 cup plain nonfat Greek yogurt

⅔ cup finely chopped cucumber

¾ teaspoon salt, divided

1 pound salmon fillet, cut into 4 pieces

2 teaspoons honey

1 teaspoon Dijon mustard

¼ teaspoon curry powder

1. Combine yogurt, cucumber and ¼ teaspoon salt in medium bowl; cover and refrigerate.

2. Preheat broiler. Line baking sheet with foil. Place salmon, skin side down, on prepared baking sheet.

3. Stir honey, mustard, curry powder and remaining ½ teaspoon salt in small bowl until smooth. Spread on salmon. Broil about 5 inches from heat 10 minutes or until opaque in center. Serve with cucumber yogurt.

PER SERVING
calories *252*
total fat *12g*
saturated fat *3g*
carbs *9g*
dietary fiber *0g*
protein *26g*

Greek Chicken Burgers

MAKES 4 SERVINGS (1 BURGER AND ¼ OF SAUCE PER SERVING)

½ cup plus 2 tablespoons plain nonfat Greek yogurt

½ medium cucumber, peeled, seeded and finely chopped

Juice of ½ lemon

3 cloves garlic, minced, divided

2 teaspoons finely chopped fresh mint *or* ½ teaspoon dried mint

½ teaspoon salt, divided

⅛ teaspoon ground white pepper

1 pound ground chicken

¾ cup (3 ounces) crumbled reduced-fat feta cheese

4 large kalamata olives, rinsed, patted dry and minced

1 egg

½ to 1 teaspoon dried oregano

¼ teaspoon black pepper

Mixed baby lettuce (optional)

Fresh mint leaves (optional)

1. Combine yogurt, cucumber, lemon juice, 2 cloves garlic, 2 teaspoons chopped mint, ¼ teaspoon salt and white pepper in medium bowl; mix well. Cover and refrigerate until ready to serve.

2. Combine chicken, cheese, olives, egg, oregano, black pepper and remaining ¼ teaspoon salt and 1 clove garlic in large bowl; mix well. Shape mixture into four patties.

3. Spray grill pan with nonstick cooking spray; heat over medium-high heat. Grill patties 5 to 7 minutes per side or until cooked through (165°F).

4. Serve burgers with sauce and mixed greens, if desired. Garnish with mint leaves.

Coq au Vin

MAKES 6 SERVINGS

½ cup all-purpose flour

1¼ teaspoons salt

¾ teaspoon black pepper

3½ to 4 pounds bone-in chicken pieces

2 tablespoons butter

8 ounces cremini mushrooms, cut in half if large

4 cloves garlic, minced

¾ cup chicken broth

¾ cup dry red wine

2 teaspoons dried thyme

1 pound red potatoes, quartered

2 carrots, sliced

2 cups frozen pearl onions (about 8 ounces)

Fresh thyme or chopped fresh parsley (optional)

1. Preheat oven to 350°F.

2. Combine flour, salt and pepper in large resealable food storage bag. Add chicken, two pieces at a time. Seal bag; shake to coat. Repeat with remaining chicken. Reserve remaining flour mixture.

3. Melt butter in Dutch oven over medium-high heat. Brown chicken in batches in single layer in Dutch oven about 3 minutes per side. Transfer to plate; set aside.

4. Add mushrooms and garlic to Dutch oven; cook and stir 2 minutes. Sprinkle reserved flour mixture over mushroom mixture; cook and stir 1 minute. Add broth, wine and thyme; bring to a boil over high heat, stirring to scrape up browned bits. Add potatoes, carrots and onions; return to a boil. Remove from heat and add chicken, partially submerging in liquid.

5. Cover and bake about 45 minutes or until chicken is cooked through (165°F for breast meat, 180°F for dark meat), and potatoes are tender. Garnish with fresh thyme.

PER SERVING
calories *700*
total fat *24g*
saturated fat *8g*
carbs *30g*
dietary fiber *3g*
protein *81g*

Greek Roast Chicken

MAKES 8 SERVINGS

1 whole chicken (4 to 5 pounds)

3 tablespoons extra virgin olive oil, divided

2 tablespoons chopped fresh rosemary

2 cloves garlic, minced

1 lemon

Fresh rosemary sprigs

1¼ teaspoons salt, divided

½ teaspoon black pepper, divided

1 can (about 14 ounces) chicken broth, divided

2 large sweet potatoes, cut into thick wedges

1 medium red onion, cut into ¼-inch wedges

1 pound fresh asparagus spears, trimmed

1. Preheat oven to 425°F. Place chicken, breast side up, in shallow roasting pan.

2. Combine 2 tablespoons oil, chopped rosemary and garlic in small bowl; brush over chicken.

3. Grate lemon peel; measure 1 teaspoon and set aside. Cut lemon into quarters; squeeze juice over chicken and place rinds and rosemary sprigs in chicken cavity. Sprinkle ¾ teaspoon salt and ¼ teaspoon pepper over chicken. Pour 1 cup broth into bottom of roasting pan; roast 30 minutes.

4. *Reduce oven temperature to 375°F.* Arrange sweet potatoes and onion wedges in single layer around chicken in roasting pan. Drizzle remaining broth and 1 tablespoon oil over vegetables; roast 15 minutes.

5. Arrange asparagus spears in roasting pan. Sprinkle remaining ½ teaspoon salt and ¼ teaspoon pepper over vegetables. Roast 10 minutes or until chicken is cooked through (165°F) and vegetables are tender. Transfer chicken to carving board. Tent with foil; let stand 10 to 15 minutes.

6. Sprinkle reserved lemon peel over chicken. Serve chicken with vegetables and pan juices.

Mediterranean Red Snapper

MAKES 4 SERVINGS

1 to 1½ pounds red snapper fillets (4 to 5 ounces each)

4 sheets (18×12 inches each) heavy-duty foil, lightly sprayed with nonstick cooking spray

8 sun-dried tomatoes, packed in oil, drained and chopped

⅓ cup sliced pitted black olives

1½ teaspoons minced garlic

½ teaspoon dried oregano

½ teaspoon dried marjoram

¼ teaspoon salt

¼ teaspoon black pepper

1. Prepare grill for direct cooking.

2. Place 1 fish fillet in center of 1 sheet of foil. Repeat with remaining fish and foil.

3. Combine sun-dried tomatoes, olives, garlic, oregano, marjoram, salt and pepper in medium bowl. Sprinkle over fish.

4. Double-fold sides and ends of foil to seal packets, leaving head space for heat circulation. Place packets on baking sheet.

5. Slide packets off baking sheet onto grid. Grill, covered, over medium-high heat 9 to 11 minutes or until fish flakes when tested with fork. Carefully open one end of each packet to allow steam to escape. Open packets and transfer mixture to serving plates.

PER SERVING
calories *210*
total fat *9g*
saturated fat *2g*
carbs *3g*
dietary fiber *1g*
protein *27g*

Baked Chicken and Garlic Orzo

MAKES 4 SERVINGS

2 teaspoons extra virgin olive oil

4 skinless bone-in chicken breast halves

1 cup chopped onions

4 cloves garlic, minced

¼ cup dry white wine

10 ounces uncooked orzo pasta

1 can (about 14 ounces) chicken broth

¼ cup water

2 tablespoons chopped fresh parsley

1 teaspoon salt

1 teaspoon dried oregano

Paprika

1 teaspoon lemon pepper

1 lemon, cut into 8 wedges

1. Preheat oven to 350°F. Heat oil in large skillet over medium-high heat. Add chicken, meat side down; cook 1 to 2 minutes or until lightly browned. Transfer chicken to plate.

2. Add onions; cook and stir 5 minutes or until softened. Add garlic; cook and stir 1 minute. Add wine, stirring to scrape up browned bits. Cook 30 seconds or until slightly reduced.

3. Spray 9-inch square baking pan with nonstick cooking spray. Add orzo, broth, water, parsley, salt and oregano. Stir in wine mixture. Place chicken breasts on top. Sprinkle lightly with paprika and lemon pepper.

4. Bake, uncovered, 1 hour 10 minutes or until chicken is cooked through and orzo is tender. Serve with fresh lemon wedges.

Lemon Rosemary Shrimp and Vegetable Souvlaki

MAKES 4 KABOBS (1 KABOB AND 1 TABLESPOON SAUCE PER SERVING)

8 ounces large raw shrimp, peeled and deveined (with tails on)

1 medium zucchini, halved lengthwise and cut into ½-inch slices

½ medium red bell pepper, cut into 1-inch squares

8 green onions, trimmed and cut into 2-inch pieces

2 tablespoons extra virgin olive oil

2 tablespoons lemon juice

2 teaspoons grated lemon peel

2 medium cloves garlic, minced

½ teaspoon salt

½ teaspoon minced fresh rosemary

⅛ teaspoon red pepper flakes

1. Prepare grill for direct cooking. Spray grid or grill pan with nonstick cooking spray.

2. Spray four 12-inch bamboo or metal skewers with cooking spray. (If using bamboo skewers, soak in water 20 to 30 minutes before using to prevent them from burning.) Alternately thread shrimp, zucchini, bell pepper and green onions onto skewers. Spray lightly with cooking spray.

3. Combine oil, lemon juice, lemon peel, garlic, salt, rosemary and red pepper flakes in small bowl; mix well.

4. Grill skewers over high heat 2 minutes per side. Remove to large serving platter; drizzle with sauce.

NOTE: "Souvlaki" is the Greek word for shishkebab. Souvlaki traditionally consists of fish or meat that has been seasoned in a mixture of oil, lemon juice, and seasonings. Many souvlaki recipes, including this one, also include chunks of vegetables such as bell pepper and onion.

PER SERVING
calories *130*
total fat *8g*
saturated fat *1g*
carbs *6g*
dietary fiber *2g*
protein *9g*

Seafood Niçoise

MAKES 4 SERVINGS

2 tablespoons extra virgin olive oil

1 leek, white part only, sliced (1 cup)

2 shallots, chopped

6 to 8 small red potatoes, cut into quarters

1 can (15 ounces) tomato purée

1 to 1½ cups bottled clam juice, divided

1 teaspoon salt

1 teaspoon herbes de Provence*

¼ teaspoon dried tarragon leaves

1 pound sea scallops or tuna, cut into 1-inch pieces

½ cup sliced pitted black olives

½ cup frozen French-cut string beans (optional)

Or substitute ¼ teaspoon each dried sage, crushed dried rosemary, thyme, oregano, marjoram and basil leaves.

1. Heat oil in large saucepan or Dutch oven over medium-high heat. Add leek and shallots; cook and stir 5 minutes or until softened. Add potatoes; cook 10 minutes, stirring occasionally. Stir in tomato purée, 1 cup clam juice, salt and herbs. Bring to a boil over high heat. Reduce heat to low. Cover and simmer 40 minutes or until potatoes are fork-tender.

2. If sauce is too thick, add remaining ½ cup clam juice. Add scallops, olives and beans, if desired. Cover and simmer 5 to 6 minutes or until scallops are opaque.

PER SERVING
calories *500*
total fat *11g*
saturated fat *2g*
carbs *79g*
dietary fiber *12g*
protein *25g*

Persian Roast Chicken with Walnut-Pomegranate Sauce

MAKES 6 SERVINGS

1 tablespoon ground cumin

1 tablespoon lemon juice

2 teaspoons grated lemon peel

1 teaspoon salt

1 teaspoon ground turmeric

¼ teaspoon saffron threads, lightly crushed

¼ teaspoon black pepper

⅛ teaspoon ground cinnamon

1 whole chicken (about 5 pounds), cut into 8 pieces

2 tablespoons extra virgin olive oil

WALNUT-POMEGRANATE SAUCE

2 cups thinly sliced onions

2 cups unsweetened pomegranate juice

½ cup sugar

½ teaspoon ground cumin

⅛ teaspoon saffron threads, lightly crushed

¼ cup walnuts, finely chopped

¼ teaspoon salt

¼ teaspoon black pepper

Pomegranate seeds (optional)

1. Preheat oven to 375°F. Spray shallow roasting pan with nonstick scooking spray.

2. Combine 1 tablespoon cumin, lemon juice, lemon peel, 1 teaspoon salt, turmeric, ¼ teaspoon saffron, ¼ teaspoon pepper and cinnamon in mall bowl; mix well to form paste. Rub mixture over chicken to lightly coat. Heat oil in large skillet over medium-high heat. Add chicken, in batches if necessary, and cook until lightly browned, about 4 minutes per side. Transfer to prepared pan.

3. Roast 25 to 28 minutes or until thermometer inserted into thickest part of each piece registers 165°F.

4. Meanwhile for sauce, heat skillet over medium-high heat. Add onions; cook and stir 8 to 10 minutes or until golden brown. Add pomegranate juice, sugar, ½ teaspoon cumin and ⅛ teaspoon saffron; bring to a boil. Cook 10 to 11 minutes or until mixture is syrupy and reduced by about half, stirring occasionally. Remove from heat. Stir in walnuts; season with ¼ teaspoon salt and ¼ teaspoon pepper.

5. Serve chicken with sauce and garnish with pomegranate seeds.

PER SERVING
calories *770*
total fat *22g*
saturated fat *4g*
carbs *33g*
dietary fiber *4g*
protein *108g*

Spiced Chicken Skewers with Yogurt-Tahini Sauce

MAKES 8 SERVINGS

1 cup plain nonfat or regular Greek yogurt

¼ cup chopped fresh parsley, plus additional for garnish

¼ cup tahini

2 tablespoons lemon juice

1 clove garlic

¾ teaspoon salt, divided

1 tablespoon vegetable oil

2 teaspoons garam masala

1 pound boneless skinless chicken breasts, cut into 1-inch pieces

1. Spray grid with nonstick cooking spray. Prepare grill for direct cooking.

2. For sauce, combine yogurt, ¼ cup parsley, tahini, lemon juice, garlic and ¼ teaspoon salt in food processor or blender; process until smooth. Set aside.

3. Combine oil, garam masala and remaining ½ teaspoon salt in medium bowl. Add chicken; toss to coat. Thread chicken on eight 6-inch bamboo or metal skewers. (If using bamboo skewers, soak in water 20 to 30 minutes before using to prevent them from burning.)

4. Grill chicken skewers over medium-high heat 5 minutes per side or until chicken is no longer pink. Serve with sauce. Garnish with additional parsley.

PER SERVING
calories *145*
total fat *7g*
saturated fat *1g*
carbs *4g*
dietary fiber *0g*
protein *16g*

Lemon-Garlic Salmon with Tzatziki Sauce

MAKES 4 SERVINGS

½ cup diced cucumber

¾ teaspoon salt, divided

1 cup plain nonfat Greek yogurt

2 tablespoons fresh lemon juice, divided

1 teaspoon grated lemon peel, divided

1 teaspoon minced garlic, divided

¼ teaspoon black pepper

4 skinless salmon fillets (4 ounces each)

1. Place cucumber in small colander set over small bowl; sprinkle with ¼ teaspoon salt. Drain 1 hour.

2. For tzatziki sauce, stir yogurt, cucumber, 1 tablespoon lemon juice, ½ teaspoon lemon peel, ½ teaspoon garlic and ¼ teaspoon salt in small bowl until combined. Cover and refrigerate until ready to use.

3. Combine remaining 1 tablespoon lemon juice, ½ teaspoon lemon peel, ½ teaspoon garlic, ¼ teaspoon salt and pepper in small bowl; mix well. Rub evenly onto salmon.

4. Heat nonstick grill pan over medium-high heat. Cook salmon 5 minutes per side or until fish begins to flake when tested with fork. Serve with tzatziki sauce.

PER SERVING
calories *243*
total fat *12g*
saturated fat *2g*
carbs *3g*
dietary fiber *0g*
protein *29g*

Easy Chicken Couscous

MAKES 6 SERVINGS

2 tablespoons extra virgin olive oil

1 onion, chopped

1 pound chicken tenders

2½ cups water

½ teaspoon salt

1 package (10 ounces) uncooked couscous

1 can (about 14 ounces) diced tomatoes with garlic

1 can (about 15 ounces) chickpeas, rinsed and drained

¼ teaspoon ground cinnamon

¼ teaspoon ground cumin

1 cup frozen peas

¼ teaspoon hot pepper sauce

1. Heat oil in large skillet over medium-high heat. Add onion; cook and stir 3 minutes or until translucent. Add chicken; cook and stir 5 minutes.

2. Meanwhile, bring water and salt to a boil in medium saucepan. Add couscous; cover and remove from heat. Let stand 10 minutes.

3. Add tomatoes, chickpeas, cinnamon and cumin to chicken mixture; mix well. Reduce heat to medium-low; cover and cook 5 minutes, stirring occasionally. Add peas and hot pepper sauce; cover and cook 5 minutes or until chicken is no longer pink in center.

4. Fluff couscous with fork; serve with chicken mixture.

PER SERVING
calories *470*
total fat *20g*
saturated fat *5g*
carbs *42g*
dietary fiber *3g*
protein *30g*

BREADS
& SANDWICHES

Quick Greek Pitas
MAKES 6 SERVINGS

1 pound ground turkey or beef

1 package (10 ounces) frozen chopped spinach, thawed and well drained

4 green onions, chopped

1 can (2¼ ounces) sliced black olives, drained

1 teaspoon dried oregano, divided

½ teaspoon salt

¼ teaspoon black pepper

1 large tomato, diced

1 cup plain nonfat Greek yogurt

½ cup mayonnaise

6 (6-inch) pita breads, warmed
  Lettuce leaves

1 cup (4 ounces) crumbled feta cheese

1. Brown turkey in large skillet over medium-high heat 6 to 8 minutes, stirring to break up meat. Add spinach, green onions, olives, ½ teaspoon oregano, salt and pepper; cook and stir 2 minutes. Stir in tomato.

2. Combine yogurt, mayonnaise and remaining ½ teaspoon oregano in small bowl. Split open pita breads; line each with lettuce leaf. Stir cheese into turkey mixture and divide among pita pockets. Serve with yogurt sauce.

Whole Wheat Focaccia

MAKES 8 SERVINGS

2 cups all-purpose flour

1¾ cups whole wheat flour

3 teaspoons Italian seasoning, divided

1 package (¼ ounce) active dry yeast (2¼ teaspoons)

1 teaspoon salt

1½ cups warm water

3 tablespoons extra virgin olive oil, divided

¼ cup shredded Parmesan cheese

1. Combine all-purpose flour, whole wheat flour, 1½ teaspoons Italian seasoning, yeast and salt in large bowl. Make a well in center; stir in water and 1 tablespoon oil until soft, sticky dough forms. Or mix with electric mixer at medium-low speed until soft dough forms.

2. Place remaining 2 tablespoons oil in 13×9-inch baking pan. Place dough in pan; turn to coat with oil. Pat and stretch dough to edges of pan. Cover and let rise in warm place 1 hour or until doubled in size.

3. Preheat oven to 400°F. Uncover dough. Dimple top with fingertips; sprinkle with remaining 1½ teaspoons Italian seasoning and cheese.

4. Bake 20 to 25 minutes or until top is golden brown and bread sounds hollow when tapped. Remove from pan; cool on wire rack. Cut into squares to serve.

PER SERVING
calories *320*
total fat *7g*
saturated fat *2g*
carbs *52g*
dietary fiber *7g*
protein *11g*

Pita Bread

MAKES 8 PITA BREADS

3½ cups all-purpose flour

1 tablespoon salt

1 tablespoon sugar

1 package (¼ ounce) instant or
   active dry yeast
   (2¼ teaspoons)

1½ cups warm water (120°F)

2 tablespoons extra virgin
   olive oil

1. Combine flour, salt, sugar and yeast in large bowl; whisk until well blended. Add 1½ cups water and oil; stir with wooden spoon until rough dough forms. If dough appears too dry, add additional 1 to 2 tablespoons water. Knead on lightly floured surface 5 to 7 minutes or until dough is smooth and elastic. Or knead with electric mixer using dough hook at low speed 5 minutes.

2. Shape dough into a ball. Place dough in greased bowl; turn to grease top. Cover and let rise in warm place 1 hour or until doubled in size.

3. Preheat oven to 500°F. Turn out dough onto lightly floured surface; press into circle. Cut dough into eight wedges. Roll each wedge into a smooth ball; flatten slightly. Let rest 10 minutes.

4. Roll each ball into a circle about ¼ inch thick. Place on two ungreased baking sheets.

5. Bake one baking sheet at a time 5 minutes or until pitas are puffed and set. Remove to wire rack to cool slightly.

Italian Pull-Apart Rolls

MAKES 15 ROLLS

3¾ cups bread flour, divided

1½ tablespoons sugar

1 package (¼ ounce) active dry yeast (2¼ teaspoons)

1½ teaspoons salt

¾ cup warm water (120°F)

½ cup warm milk (120°F)

2 tablespoons extra virgin olive oil

¾ cup grated Parmesan cheese

2 teaspoons Italian seasoning

⅓ cup butter, melted

1. Combine 1½ cups flour, sugar, yeast and salt in large bowl of stand mixer. Add warm water, milk and oil; beat with paddle attachment at medium speed 3 minutes.

2. Replace paddle attachment with dough hook. Add 2 cups flour; mix at low speed to form firm dough. Add enough remaining flour, 1 tablespoon at a time, if necessary to prevent sticking. Mix at low speed 5 minutes.

3. Shape dough into a ball. Place dough in greased bowl; turn to grease top. Cover and let rise in warm place about 30 minutes or until doubled in size.

4. Grease 2½-quart baking dish. Combine cheese and Italian seasoning in shallow bowl. Place melted butter in another shallow bowl.

5. Turn out dough onto lightly floured surface; roll gently into 20-inch rope. Cut dough into 15 pieces; roll each piece into a ball. Dip balls in melted butter; roll in cheese mixture to coat. Place in prepared baking dish; cover and let rise about 30 minutes or until doubled in size. Preheat oven to 375°F.

6. Bake about 30 minutes or until rolls are golden brown. Cool in baking dish on wire rack 10 minutes. Serve warm.

PER SERVING
calories *210*
total fat *9g*
saturated fat *9g*
carbs *27g*
dietary fiber *1g*
protein *7g*

Tomato and Cheese Focaccia

MAKES 8 SERVINGS

1 package (¼ ounce) active dry yeast (2¼ teaspoons)

¾ cup warm water (120°F)

2 cups all-purpose flour

½ teaspoon salt

4½ tablespoons extra virgin olive oil, divided

1 teaspoon Italian seasoning

8 oil-packed sun-dried tomatoes, well drained

½ cup (2 ounces) shredded provolone cheese

¼ cup grated Parmesan cheese

1. Dissolve yeast in warm water in small bowl; let stand 5 minutes or until bubbly. Combine flour and salt in food processor. Add yeast mixture and 3 tablespoons oil; process until dough forms a ball. Process 1 minute.

2. Turn dough out onto lightly floured surface. Knead about 2 minutes or until dough is smooth and elastic. Shape dough into a ball. Place dough in greased bowl; turn to grease top. Cover and let rise in warm place about 30 minutes or until doubled in size.

3. Brush 10-inch round cake pan, deep-dish pizza pan or springform pan with ½ tablespoon oil. Punch down dough; let rest 5 minutes.

4. Press dough into prepared pan. Brush with remaining 1 tablespoon oil; sprinkle with Italian seasoning. Press sun-dried tomatoes into top of dough; sprinkle with provolone and Parmesan. Cover and let rise in warm place 15 minutes. Preheat oven to 425°F.

5. Bake 20 to 25 minutes or until golden brown. Cut into wedges.

   NOTE: If mixing dough by hand, combine flour and salt in large bowl. Stir in yeast mixture and 3 tablespoons oil until a ball forms. Turn out onto lightly floured surface and knead about 10 minutes or until smooth and elastic. Or use an electric mixer fitted with the dough hook to knead the dough. Knead on medium-low speed 5 minutes or until dough is smooth and elastic. Proceed as directed.

PER SERVING
calories *230*
total fat *12g*
saturated fat *3g*
carbs *25g*
dietary fiber *1g*
protein *7g*

Savory Pita Chips

MAKES 4 SERVINGS (6 CHIPS PER SERVING)

2 whole wheat or white pita breads

Olive oil cooking spray

3 tablespoons grated Parmesan cheese

1 teaspoon dried basil

¼ teaspoon garlic powder

1. Preheat oven to 350°F. Line baking sheet with foil.

2. Carefully split each pita round in half horizontally into two rounds. Cut each round into six wedges.

3. Place wedges, inside layer down, on prepared baking sheet. Spray with nonstick cooking spray. Turn over; spray again.

4. Combine cheese, basil and garlic powder in small bowl; sprinkle evenly over pita wedges.

5. Bake 12 to 14 minutes or until golden brown. Cool completely.

PER SERVING
calories *108*
total fat *2g*
saturated fat *3g*
carbs *18g*
dietary fiber *2g*
protein *5g*

Cucumber and Chickpea Pita Sandwiches

MAKES 4 SERVINGS

1 cup plain nonfat Greek yogurt

1 tablespoon chopped fresh cilantro

2 cloves garlic, minced

1 teaspoon lemon juice

1 can (about 15 ounces) chickpeas, rinsed and drained

1 can (14 ounces) artichoke hearts, rinsed, drained and coarsely chopped

1½ cups thinly sliced cucumber halves (halved lengthwise)

½ cup shredded carrot

½ cup chopped green onions

4 whole wheat pita breads, cut in half

1. Combine yogurt, cilantro, garlic and lemon juice in small bowl; mix well.

2. Combine chickpeas, artichoke hearts, cucumbers, carrot and green onions in medium bowl. Stir in yogurt mixture until well blended. Divide cucumber mixture among pita halves.

Socca (Niçoise Chickpea Pancake)

MAKES 6 SERVINGS

1 cup chickpea flour

¾ teaspoon salt

½ teaspoon black pepper

1 cup water

5 tablespoons extra virgin olive oil, divided

1½ teaspoons minced fresh basil *or* ½ teaspoon dried basil

1 teaspoon minced fresh rosemary *or* ¼ teaspoon dried rosemary

¼ teaspoon dried thyme

1. Sift chickpea flour into medium bowl. Stir in salt and pepper. Gradually whisk in water until smooth. Stir in 2 tablespoons oil. Let stand at least 30 minutes.

2. Preheat oven to 450°F. Place 9- or 10-inch cast iron skillet in oven to heat.

3. Add basil, rosemary and thyme to batter; whisk until smooth. Carefully remove skillet from oven. Add 2 tablespoons oil to skillet, swirling to coat pan evenly. Immediately pour in batter.

4. Bake 12 to 15 minutes or until edge of pancake begins to pull away from side of pan and center is firm. Remove from oven. Preheat broiler.

5. Brush with remaining 1 tablespoon oil. Broil 2 to 4 minutes or until dark brown in spots. Cut into wedges. Serve warm.

TIP: Socca are pancakes made of chickpea flour and are commonly served in paper cones as a savory street food in the south of France, especially around Nice.

PER SERVING
calories *160*
total fat *12g*
saturated fat *2g*
carbs *9g*
dietary fiber *2g*
protein *3g*

Olive and Herb Focaccia

MAKES 2 FOCACCIA BREADS (24 SERVINGS)

3½ to 3¾ cups bread flour

1¼ cups warm water (120°F)

½ cup extra virgin olive oil, divided

1 package (¼ ounce) active dry yeast (2¼ teaspoons)

2 teaspoons honey

1 teaspoon salt

1 cup chopped pitted kalamata olives

3 tablespoons chopped fresh rosemary

2 tablespoons chopped fresh thyme

3 cloves garlic, minced

Black pepper

¼ cup grated Romano cheese

1. Combine 3½ cups flour, warm water, 3 tablespoons oil, yeast, honey and salt in large bowl of stand mixer. Mix with dough hook at low speed 2 minutes or until soft dough forms, adding additional flour, 1 tablespoon at a time, if necessary to clean side of bowl. Knead 5 minutes or until dough is smooth and elastic.

2. Shape dough into a ball. Place dough in greased bowl; turn to grease top. Cover and let rise in warm place about 1 hour or until doubled in size.

3. Preheat oven to 450°F. Brush each of two 9-inch cake pans or deep-dish pizza pans with 1 tablespoon oil. Divide dough in half. Roll out each half into 9-inch circle on lightly floured surface. Place dough in prepared pans; cover and let rest 10 minutes.

4. Make indentations in top of dough with fingertips or handle of wooden spoon. Sprinkle evenly with olives, rosemary, thyme and garlic; drizzle with remaining 3 tablespoons oil. Sprinkle with pepper.

5. Bake about 15 minutes or until lightly browned. Immediately sprinkle with cheese. Remove to wire racks to cool slightly. Serve warm.

PER SERVING
calories *114*
total fat *8g*
saturated fat *1g*
carbs *14g*
dietary fiber *1g*
protein *2g*

Chicken Kabobs in Pita Bread

¼ cup extra virgin olive oil

¼ cup lemon juice

½ teaspoon salt

½ teaspoon dried oregano

¼ teaspoon garlic powder

⅛ teaspoon black pepper

2 boneless skinless chicken breasts (about 8 ounces), cut into 1-inch cubes

2 large pita breads

1 small onion, thinly sliced

1 tomato, thinly sliced

½ cup plain Greek yogurt

Chopped fresh parsley (optional)

1. Mix oil, lemon juice, salt, oregano, garlic powder and pepper in medium bowl. Add chicken to oil mixture; toss to coat. Cover and refrigerate at least 3 hours or overnight.

2. Preheat broiler. Spray broiler pan with nonstick cooking spray. Remove chicken from marinade, reserving marinade. Thread chicken onto four small metal skewers.

3. Broil kabobs about 5 inches from heat 8 to 10 minutes or until chicken is golden, brushing frequently with marinade. Turn kabobs and brush with marinade. Broil 5 to 7 minutes or until chicken is cooked through.

4. Cut each pita bread in half; gently pull each half open to form pocket. Remove chicken from kabobs and place inside pita pockets; top with onion, tomato, yogurt and parsley, if desired.

PER SERVING
calories *305*
total fat *15g*
saturated fat *2g*
carbs *24g*
dietary fiber *2g*
protein *19g*

Chicken and Roasted Tomato Panini

MAKES 4 SERVINGS

12 ounces plum tomatoes (about 2 large), cut into ⅛-inch slices

½ teaspoon coarse salt, divided

¼ teaspoon black pepper, divided

2 tablespoons olive oil, divided

4 boneless skinless chicken breasts (about 4 ounces each)

3 tablespoons butter, softened

¼ teaspoon garlic powder

¼ cup mayonnaise

2 tablespoons pesto sauce

8 slices sourdough or rustic Italian bread

4 slices (about 1 ounce each) provolone cheese, cut in half

½ cup baby spinach

1. Preheat oven to 400°F. Line baking sheet with parchment paper. Arrange tomato slices in single layer on prepared baking sheet. Sprinkle with ¼ teaspoon salt and ⅛ teaspoon pepper; drizzle with 1 tablespoon oil. Roast 25 minutes or until tomatoes are softened and begin to caramelize around edges.

2. Meanwhile, prepare chicken. If chicken breasts are thicker than ½ inch, pound to ½-inch thickness. Heat remaining 1 tablespoon oil in large skillet over medium-high heat. Season both sides of chicken with remaining ¼ teaspoon salt and ⅛ teaspoon pepper. Add to skillet; cook about 6 minutes per side or until golden brown and cooked through (165°F). Remove to plate; let stand 10 minutes before slicing. Cut diagonally into ½-inch slices.

3. Combine butter and garlic powder in small bowl; mix well. Combine mayonnaise and pesto in another small bowl; mix well.

4. Spread one side of each bread slice with garlic butter. For each sandwich, place 1 bread slice, buttered side down, on plate. Spread with generous 1 tablespoon pesto mayonnaise. Layer with half a cheese slice, 4 to 5 roasted tomato slices, 4 to 6 spinach leaves, 1 sliced chicken breast, another half of cheese slice and 4 to 6 spinach leaves. Top with second bread slice, buttered side up.

5. Preheat panini press, indoor grill or grill pan. Cook sandwiches until bread is golden brown and cheese is melted.

PER SERVING
calories *700*
total fat *43g*
saturated fat *14g*
carbs *41g*
dietary fiber *1g*
protein *40g*

Eggplant, Goat Cheese and Olive Pizza
MAKES 4 SERVINGS

⅔ cup warm water (120°F)

½ (¼-ounce) package instant or active dry yeast

1 teaspoon sugar

1¾ cups all-purpose or bread flour

½ teaspoon salt

1 small eggplant, cut into ¼-inch-thick slices

1 tablespoon extra virgin olive oil

¼ cup finely chopped onion

1 tablespoon minced fresh rosemary leaves *or* 2 teaspoons dried rosemary

3 cloves garlic, minced

½ cup roasted red peppers

2 ounces goat cheese, crumbled

6 kalamata olives, pitted and halved

1. For crust, combine water, yeast and sugar in large bowl; stir to dissolve yeast. Let stand 5 to 10 minutes or until foamy.

2. Stir in flour and salt until soft dough forms. Knead on lightly floured surface 5 minutes or until dough is smooth and elastic, adding additional flour, 1 tablespoon at a time, as needed. Place dough in medium greased bowl; turn to grease top. Cover and let rise in warm place 30 minutes or until doubled in size.

3. Punch dough down; shape into 7-inch disc. Let rest 2 to 3 minutes. Pat and gently stretch dough from edges until dough will not stretch anymore. Let rest 3 minutes. Continue patting and stretching until dough is 12 to 14 inches in diameter. Spray pizza pan or baking sheet with nonstick cooking spray; press dough into pan.

4. Preheat oven to 500°F. Spray baking sheet with cooking spray. Place eggplant slices on baking sheet; spray with cooking spray. Bake 8 to 10 minutes or until light golden. Turn slices; bake 6 to 8 minutes or until golden and very tender. Bake pizza crust 3 to 4 minutes or until top is crisp and beginning to brown.

5. Heat oil in small skillet over medium heat. Add onion, rosemary and garlic; cook and stir 3 minutes or until onion is translucent.

6. Process roasted pepper strips in food processor until smooth; spread evenly over baked crust, leaving 1-inch border. Arrange eggplant on top, slightly overlapping slices; sprinkle with onion mixture. Top with cheese and olives.

7. Bake 3 to 5 minutes or until crust is deep golden.

Shrimp, Chickpea and Tabbouleh Pockets

1 cup diced tomatoes

1 cup drained canned chickpeas

1 package (7 ounces) prepared tabbouleh*

¼ pound cooked small shrimp, tails removed, chopped

2 whole wheat pita breads

Prepared tabbouleh can be found in most grocery stores; it is usually located near the refrigerated hummus. If you can't find prepared tabbouleh, prepare a 5- or 6-ounce package of tabbouleh mix according to package directions.

1. Combine tomatoes, chickpeas, tabbouleh and shrimp in medium bowl; mix well.

2. Wrap pita breads in paper towel; microwave on HIGH 10 seconds. Cut pitas in half; fill with tabbouleh mixture.

PER SERVING
calories *234*
total fat *6g*
saturated fat *1g*
carbs *34g*
dietary fiber *7g*
protein *14g*

Mediterranean Roasted Vegetable Wraps

MAKES 4 SERVINGS

1 head cauliflower, cut into 1-inch florets

4 tablespoons extra virgin olive oil, divided

2 teaspoons ras el hanout, 7-spice blend, shawarma blend or za'atar

1 teaspoon salt, divided

1 zucchini, quartered lengthwise and cut into ¼-inch pieces

1 yellow squash, quartered lengthwise and cut into ¼-inch pieces

½ red onion, thinly sliced

¼ cup red pepper sauce (avjar)

4 large thin pita breads or lavash (10 inches)

4 ounces feta cheese, crumbled

1 cup drained canned chickpeas

¼ cup diced tomatoes

¼ cup minced fresh parsley

¼ cup diced cucumber (optional)

2 teaspoons vegetable oil

1. Preheat oven to 400°F. Combine cauliflower, 2 tablespoons olive oil, ras el hanout and ½ teaspoon salt in large bowl; toss to coat. Spread on half of sheet pan. Combine zucchini, yellow squash, onion, remaining 2 tablespoons olive oil and ½ teaspoon salt in same bowl; toss to coat. Spread on other side of sheet pan. Roast 25 minutes or until vegetables are browned and tender, stirring once. Remove from oven; cool slightly.

2. Spread 1 tablespoon red pepper sauce on one pita. Top with one fourth of vegetables, cheese, chickpeas, tomatoes, parsley and cucumber, if desired. Fold two sides over filling; roll up into burrito shape. Repeat with remaining ingredients.

3. Heat 1 teaspoon vegetable oil in large skillet over medium-high heat. Add two wraps, seam sides down; cook 1 minute or until browned. Turn and cook other side until browned. Repeat with remaining vegetable oil and wraps. Cut in half to serve.

PER SERVING
calories *560*
total fat *29g*
saturated fat *9g*
carbs *60g*
dietary fiber *6g*
protein *17g*

PER SERVING
calories *150*
total fat *0g*
saturated fat *0g*
carbs *38g*
dietary fiber *0g*
protein *1g*

SWEETS
& TREATS

Pomegranate Orange Sherbet

MAKES 6 SERVINGS (1 CUP EACH)

⅔ cup sugar

⅔ cup water

2 cups bottled pomegranate juice

1 cup fresh orange juice

2 teaspoons grated orange peel

2 tablespoons grenadine (optional)

1. Bring sugar and water to a boil in small saucepan over high heat, stirring to dissolve sugar. Boil 5 minutes or until syrup is slightly thickened. Cool slightly.

2. Combine pomegranate juice, orange juice, orange peel and grenadine, if desired, in medium bowl. Stir in sugar syrup. Refrigerate at least 2 hours or until cold.

3. Freeze mixture in ice cream maker according to manufacturer's directions until soft. Transfer sherbet to freezer containers. Freeze at least 2 hours or until firm. Scoop and serve.

Sautéed Pears with Maple Mascarpone Cream

MAKES 4 SERVINGS

2 **Bartlett pears**

¼ **cup water**

½ **cup mascarpone cheese**

2 **tablespoons maple syrup**

1 **tablespoon butter**

1. Peel pears; cut in half and remove cores. Place in large microwavable dish. Add water; microwave on HIGH 5 minutes or until pears are softened. Combine mascarpone cheese and maple syrup in small bowl.

2. Melt butter in large skillet over medium-low heat. Add pears; cook 5 minutes or until slightly browned on edges.

3. Place pear halves on serving dishes; top with mascarpone cream. Serve immediately.

EXTRAS: Sprinkle each serving with crushed gingerbread cookie crumbs or chopped crystallized ginger.

PER SERVING
calories *680*
total fat *29g*
saturated fat *16g*
carbs *21g*
dietary fiber *3g*
protein *5g*

Fig and Hazelnut Cake

MAKES 12 SERVINGS

¾ cup hazelnuts with skins removed (about 4 ounces), coarsely chopped

¾ cup whole dried figs (about 4 ounces), coarsely chopped

⅔ cup slivered blanched almonds (about 3 ounces), coarsely chopped

3 ounces semisweet chocolate, finely chopped

⅓ cup diced candied orange peel

⅓ cup diced candied lemon peel

1¼ cups all-purpose flour

1¾ teaspoons baking powder

¾ teaspoon salt

3 eggs

½ cup sugar

1. Preheat oven to 300°F. Grease 8×4-inch loaf pan. Combine hazelnuts, figs, almonds, chocolate and candied orange and lemon peels in medium bowl; mix well. Whisk flour, baking powder and salt in small bowl.

2. Beat eggs and sugar in large bowl with electric mixer at high speed 5 minutes or until thick and pale yellow. Gently fold in nut mixture. Sift half of flour mixture over egg mixture; gently fold until blended. Repeat with remaining flour mixture. Spread batter evenly in prepared pan.

3. Bake 60 to 70 minutes or until top is golden brown and firm to the touch. Cool in pan on wire rack 5 minutes. Remove from pan; cool completely on wire rack.

PER SERVING
calories *300*
total fat *13g*
saturated fat *3g*
carbs *44g*
dietary fiber *3g*
protein *6g*

Classic Anise Biscotti

MAKES 48 COOKIES (2 COOKIES PER SERVING)

¾ cup whole blanched almonds (about 4 ounces)

2¼ cups all-purpose flour

1 teaspoon baking powder

¾ teaspoon salt

¾ cup sugar

½ cup (1 stick) unsalted butter, softened

3 eggs

2 tablespoons brandy

2 teaspoons grated lemon peel

1 tablespoon anise seeds

1. Preheat oven to 375°F. Spread almonds in single layer on ungreased baking sheet. Bake 6 to 8 minutes or until lightly browned. Turn off oven. Let almonds cool slightly; coarsely chop.

2. Combine flour, baking powder and salt in medium bowl. Beat sugar and butter in large bowl with electric mixer at medium speed until light and fluffy. Add eggs, one at a time, beating well after each addition. Stir in brandy and lemon peel. Gradually add flour mixture, stirring until smooth. Stir in chopped almonds and anise seeds. Cover and refrigerate dough 1 hour or until firm.

3. Preheat oven to 375°F. Grease large baking sheet. Divide dough in half. Shape each half into 12×2-inch log on lightly floured surface. (Dough will be fairly soft.) Pat smooth with lightly floured fingertips. Transfer to prepared baking sheet. Bake 20 to 25 minutes or until logs are light golden brown. *Reduce oven temperature to 350°F.* Cool logs completely on wire rack.

4. Cut logs diagonally with serrated knife into ½-inch-thick slices. Place slices flat in single layer on ungreased baking sheets.

5. Bake 8 minutes. Turn slices; bake 10 to 12 minutes or until cut surfaces are lightly browned and biscotti are dry. Remove to wire racks; cool completely. Store biscotti in airtight container up to 2 weeks.

PER SERVING
calories *140*
total fat *7g*
saturated fat *3g*
carbs *17g*
dietary fiber *1g*
protein *3g*

Italian Ice

MAKES 4 SERVINGS

1 cup sugar

1 cup sweet or dry fruity
   white wine

1 cup water

1 cup lemon juice

2 egg whites*

*Use only grade A clean, uncracked
eggs, preferably pasteurized.*

1. Combine sugar, wine and water in small saucepan. Cook over medium-high heat until sugar is dissolved and syrup boils, stirring frequently. Cover; boil 1 minute. Uncover; adjust heat to maintain simmer. Simmer 10 minutes without stirring. Remove from heat. Refrigerate 1 hour or until syrup is completely cool.

2. Stir lemon juice into cooled syrup. Pour into 9-inch round cake pan. Freeze 1 hour.

3. Quickly stir mixture with fork to break up ice crystals. Freeze 1 hour more or until firm but not solid. Meanwhile, place medium bowl in freezer to chill.

4. Beat egg whites in small bowl with electric mixer at high speed until stiff peaks form. Transfer lemon mixture from pan to chilled bowl. Immediately beat lemon mixture with whisk or fork until smooth. Fold in egg whites. Spread mixture evenly into same cake pan. Freeze 30 minutes. Stir with fork; cover pan with foil. Freeze at least 3 hours or until firm.

5. Scoop into bowls to serve.

PER SERVING
calories *270*
total fat *0g*
saturated fat *0g*
carbs *56g*
dietary fiber *0g*
protein *2g*

Macédoine

MAKES 8 SERVINGS (1 CUP PER SERVING)

Finely grated peel and juice
of 1 lemon

Finely grated peel and juice
of 1 lime

8 cups diced assorted seasonal
fruits (see Note)

1 cup sweet spumante wine or
freshly squeezed orange
juice

¼ cup sugar

½ cup coarsely chopped walnuts
or almonds, toasted*

*To toast walnuts, cook in medium
skillet over medium heat 2 minutes
or until lightly browned, stirring
frequently.*

1. Combine lemon juice and lime juice in large bowl. Add fruit; toss to coat.

2. Combine wine, sugar and citrus peels in small bowl, stirring until sugar is
   dissolved. Pour over fruit mixture; toss gently. Cover; refrigerate 1 hour.

3. Sprinkle walnuts on fruit mixture just before serving.

NOTE: Apples, pears and bananas are essential fruits in a traditional Macédoine. Add
as many seasonally ripe fruits to them as you can—variety is the key. As you select
fruits, try to achieve a diversity of textures, being sure to avoid mushy, overripe
fruit.

PER SERVING

calories *169*
total fat *3g*
saturated fat *1g*
carbs *33g*
dietary fiber *4g*
protein *2g*

Apricot Dessert Soufflé

MAKES 6 SERVINGS

3 tablespoons butter

2 tablespoons all-purpose flour

¾ cup apricot fruit spread

¼ cup water

⅓ cup finely chopped dried apricots

3 egg yolks, beaten

4 egg whites

¼ teaspoon cream of tartar

⅛ teaspoon salt

Sweetened Whipped Cream (recipe follows, optional)

1. Preheat oven to 325°F. Melt butter in medium saucepan. Add flour; cook and stir until bubbly. Add fruit spread and water; cook and stir 3 minutes or until thickened. Remove from heat; whisk in egg yolks. Cool to room temperature, stirring occasionally.

2. Beat egg whites, cream of tartar and salt in small bowl at high speed with electric mixer until stiff peaks form. Gently fold into apricot mixture. Fold in apricots. Spoon into 1½-quart soufflé dish.

3. Bake 30 minutes or until puffed and golden brown.* Meanwhile, prepare Sweetened Whipped Cream, if desired; serve with soufflé.

*Soufflé will be soft in center. For a firmer soufflé, increase baking time to 35 minutes.

SWEETENED WHIPPED CREAM: Beat 1 cup cream, 2 tablespoons powdered sugar and ½ teaspoon vanilla in chilled large metal bowl with electric mixer at high speed until soft peaks form. *Do not overbeat.* Refrigerate until ready to serve. Makes about 2 cups.

PER SERVING
calories *148*
total fat *9g*
saturated fat *5g*
carbs *14g*
dietary fiber *1g*
protein *4g*

Citrus Olive Oil Cake

MAKES 10 SERVINGS

1¾ cups all-purpose flour

Grated peel of 1 orange

Grated peel of 1 lemon

1 teaspoon salt

1 teaspoon baking powder

½ teaspoon baking soda

1½ cups sugar

3 eggs

1 cup extra virgin olive oil

½ cup milk

¼ cup orange juice

2 tablespoons lemon juice

ORANGE SYRUP (OPTIONAL)

¾ cup orange juice

2 tablespoons sugar

1. Preheat oven to 350°F. Spray 9-inch springform pan or deep cake pan (at least 3 inches) with nonstick cooking spray.* Line bottom of pan with parchment paper; spray paper. Wrap bottom of springform pan with foil to catch any drips.

2. Whisk flour, orange peel, lemon peel, salt, baking powder and baking soda in small bowl.

3. Beat 1½ cups sugar and eggs in large bowl with electric mixer at medium speed 3 minutes (mixture will be pale and fluffy). With mixer running on medium-low speed, add oil in thin steady stream. Stop and scrape bowl.

4. Combine milk, ¼ cup orange juice and lemon juice in 2-cup measure. With mixer running on low speed, add milk mixture alternately with flour mixture, beating just until blended after each addition. Pour batter into prepared pan; smooth top. Bang pan on counter once to remove air bubbles.

5. Bake 50 to 55 minutes or until top is dark golden, center is no longer jiggly and toothpick inserted into center comes out clean. Cool completely in pan on wire rack. Run thin knife around edge of cake; remove side of springform pan or invert onto plate.

6. Meanwhile for orange syrup, if desired, combine ¾ cup orange juice and 2 tablespoons sugar in small saucepan; bring to a boil over medium-high heat. Reduce heat to medium; cook 10 minutes or until mixture is reduced to about ¼ cup. Cool slightly. Pour over cake.

You can also bake the cake in two regular 9-inch round cake pans instead of one deep pan. Start checking the cakes for doneness at 25 minutes.

PER SERVING

calories *420*
total fat *24g*
saturated fat *4g*
carbs *49g*
dietary fiber *1g*
protein *5g*

INDEX

Metric Conversion Chart

VOLUME MEASUREMENTS (dry)

¹/₈ teaspoon = 0.5 mL
¹/₄ teaspoon = 1 mL
¹/₂ teaspoon = 2 mL
³/₄ teaspoon = 4 mL
1 teaspoon = 5 mL
1 tablespoon = 15 mL
2 tablespoons = 30 mL
¹/₄ cup = 60 mL
¹/₃ cup = 75 mL
¹/₂ cup = 125 mL
²/₃ cup = 150 mL
³/₄ cup = 175 mL
1 cup = 250 mL
2 cups = 1 pint = 500 mL
3 cups = 750 mL
4 cups = 1 quart = 1 L

VOLUME MEASUREMENTS (fluid)

1 fluid ounce (2 tablespoons) = 30 mL
4 fluid ounces (¹/₂ cup) = 125 mL
8 fluid ounces (1 cup) = 250 mL
12 fluid ounces (1¹/₂ cups) = 375 mL
16 fluid ounces (2 cups) = 500 mL

WEIGHTS (mass)

¹/₂ ounce = 15 g
1 ounce = 30 g
3 ounces = 90 g
4 ounces = 120 g
8 ounces = 225 g
10 ounces = 285 g
12 ounces = 360 g
16 ounces = 1 pound = 450 g

DIMENSIONS

¹/₁₆ inch = 2 mm
¹/₈ inch = 3 mm
¹/₄ inch = 6 mm
¹/₂ inch = 1.5 cm
³/₄ inch = 2 cm
1 inch = 2.5 cm

OVEN TEMPERATURES

250°F = 120°C
275°F = 140°C
300°F = 150°C
325°F = 160°C
350°F = 180°C
375°F = 190°C
400°F = 200°C
425°F = 220°C
450°F = 230°C

BAKING PAN SIZES

Utensil	Size in Inches/Quarts	Metric Volume	Size in Centimeters
Baking or Cake Pan (square or rectangular)	8×8×2	2 L	20×20×5
	9×9×2	2.5 L	23×23×5
	12×8×2	3 L	30×20×5
	13×9×2	3.5 L	33×23×5
Loaf Pan	8×4×3	1.5 L	20×10×7
	9×5×3	2 L	23×13×7
Round Layer Cake Pan	8×1½	1.2 L	20×4
	9×1½	1.5 L	23×4
Pie Plate	8×1¼	750 mL	20×3
	9×1¼	1 L	23×3
Baking Dish or Casserole	1 quart	1 L	—
	1½ quart	1.5 L	—
	2 quart	2 L	—